HARD CALIBRE

HARD CALIBRE

by

Phil Riley

The Memoir Club

© Philip Riley 2013

First published in 2013

All rights reserved.
Unauthorised duplication
contravenes existing laws.
British Library Cataloguing in
Publication Data.
A catalogue record for this book
is available from the
British Library

ISBN: 978-1-84104-573-3

Printed by JASPRINT, Washington, NE37 2SH

*Dedicated to my dear wife, Maggie.
Who despite her suffering
managed to instil the required commitment in me
to reach the finish line.*

Contents

List of Illustrations ix
Acknowledgements xi
Introduction xiii
Chapter 1   At Home 1
Chapter 2   Basic Training 10
Chapter 3   An Armourer 16
Chapter 4   First Posting 26
Chapter 5   44 Squadron 33
Chapter 6   Research and Development 41
Chapter 7   90 Squadron 49
Chapter 8   With the Army 60
Chapter 9   The Knife 73
Chapter 10   Down the Cape 80
Chapter 11   Dinner at the Palace 95
Chapter 12   The Wedding 112
Chapter 13   Beaufort Inspection 119
Chapter 14   We go Paddling 128
Chapter 15   Up in the Hills 139
Chapter 16   The Imphal Valley 145
Chapter 17   The long way Home 156

List of Illustrations

1. Locations in United Kingdom 17
2. Boeing B17C also known as Flying Fortress 1 52
3. Location of Pollsmoor in 1942 84
4. The main hangar at the Aerodrome 100
5. Jodhpur Town Plan, 1933 110
6. A Bristol Beaufort similar to the ill-fated Beaufort DW941 120
7. A Hawker Hurricane Mk.IIb receiving an overhaul 149

Kenny's story is just one story that was saved unlike the tens of thousands of stories that were never told. Sometime after World War II Mr. Bill Barker, a veteran of Normandy himself, wrote a verse as a tribute to all veterans.

The Veterans

They ask us why we do it
Why we still parade
Now that we are getting older
And just a little frayed
It's not for the sake of glory,
Or the medals on our chests
It's simply that we are comrades
Who stood the final test.
On the 6th June that fateful day
A day that we will never forget
Many a lad laid down his life
And paid the final debt.
So when you see a Veteran
Give the man your hand
For the medals on his chest
Were won in foreign lands
And when God asks the question
Who are you my man
I will proudly answer
Sir, I am a Veteran.

Accredited to Bill Barker a veteran of Normandy

Lest we forget

Acknowledgements

Mr. Harold Payne, owner of the Anglia Motel, Fleet Hargrave near Holbeach was most generous in freely offering The Veterans to be included, for which I sincerely thank him. The verse is believed to have been written by Bill Barker of Kirton, himself a veteran of Normandy who gave it to Harold around 1995. For over twenty years Harold with his family, friends and staff have raised £520,000 for the Veterans association and in the last three years raised £60,000 for the Royal Anglians. Over several years Harold with his family and collegues have enabled over 1,000 Veterans return to Normandy as an act of rememberence. Efforts that are most truly remarkable.

His Highness Maharaja Umaid Singhji for offering the services of the Research Centre, Fort Jodhpur.

M. Prahlad Singh, General Manager of the Mehrangarh Museum, Fort Jodhpur for responding to my enquiries.

Mr. Spike Mayes (deceased), local author of Steeple Bumstead for being the initial appraiser of my work.

Mr. John Young B.A. Hons. Head Tutor of the Technical Authorship Course at Chippenham Technical College 1985 for being so capable in debating the finer points of English grammar.

The Cape Times, South Africa for their assistance in my research.

The National Maritime Museum, Greenwich, London for assisting with wartime convoy information.

National Geographic for supplying photographs.

Imperial War Museum for supplying photographs.

Air Team Images for a most efficient service in supplying photographs.

Public Records Office for certain dates.

Major Mathias Joost of the Royal Canadian Air Force - History and Heritage Department, for supplying detailed aircrew information.

Jacket cover by Red Side Up, Haverhill, Suffolk.

Introduction

Everyone has a tall story to tell, tucked away somewhere in their 'bag' of memories and Kenny was no exception but as we worked together he only ever got to tell me 'snippets' of the story. One week he mentioned some fights, another week he told me about aircraft crashes and a large flood in India. Yet another time he was living in luxury but then he was at deaths door with illness. After a while I tried to piece together the snippets and realised that if they were true, this man had cheated death so many times it was just amazing and so contrary to his unassuming appearance. In his late fifties with some remaining grey curly hair and about 5' 7" yet not well built after a serious illness, the only thing that belied Kenny's casual manner were his dark penetrating eyes. It was those eyes that had seen so much.

    As I pressed him harder he loosely gave me the 'joined up' version which basically covered his teen years and his service as an Armourer in the Royal Air Force. Indeed, just surviving to adulthood had been more luck than management due to the desire for occasional speed trials on motorcycles, which ended abruptly. Once he had joined up, the nature of the work and service requirements laid the field wide open and that is not overlooking the fact that aeroplanes don't always keep flying. Although we were a generation apart, we had many things in common and became good friends to the extent that during one night shift I told him that he should get the whole story written down. He replied in his basic Lancashire accent 'Ya might be right, but ahm not one for writing much' in a very matter of fact tone. It's peculiar how naivety is only evident with hindsight. 'Look.' I said, somewhat enthused. 'I'll write it for you.' He looked at me 'You reckon?' 'Yeh, sure' I replied. I'd taken a moment's thought now 'but I'll have to ask you a lot of questions.' He thought a moment 'Ah suppose so. Go on then.' So it was that on one night shift at Ross Foods Ltd. Westwick in the early hours of the morning I committed myself to an amount of work that I had previously thought incomprehensible. Over the next few months and years I frequently visited Kenny at his home where I asked questions and interviewed him then returned to my home and produced loads of notes about all he had said. This continued until the toll of lifes tribulations forced me to abandon the project which permanently scarred my conscience. When I was informed of his death some years later, I was truly grieved and the scar was freshly torn. When my wife and I went to Norwich and formed fifty percent of the mourners at his cremation, after his wife and daughter, I had to address my inner torment. In some effort of self redemption for failing to keep my word, I resolved to fulfill my original promise to him, regardless of the time or cost by making an absolute commitment to myself this time, to write Kenny's story.

CHAPTER ONE

At Home

Timing has never been a strong point of mine and certainly not a positive one. If marks were awarded for negative timing abilities, I would be in the front runners. In 1939 there were only two 'timings' that not only would I never forget but would be engraved upon my mind as if they had been on stone. The first resulted in me doing one of my all too rare good deeds but the second just sends a shiver down my spine.

In 1937 my father retired, mainly due to ill health from building railways along the 'gold and Ivory coast' somewhere in Africa, known as the 'white man's' grave due to the diseases that killed them off but this was all I ever knew. He was very fortunate really as he ended up as Foreman Plate Layer and on his final return in 1937, after a couple of months recovery from a bout of Yellow Fever he was in a position to purchase the Commercial Hotel at Upper Mill which was more or less next to our village of Swinton. When they actually moved there, because I was established with my job at the chemists with my motorcycle, a 350cc Raleigh and my friends in the area which I loved, I chose to stay with my school mate Walter Bailey. Walter and I had been really good mates at school. They were OK with that. I think I was just growing up a bit.

The arrangement seemed pretty good for both of us as he was a good friend and had a similar outlook to myself. So for about the one and a half years following, life was certainly not a hardship. We both had to work for a living but come the weekends we were nicely located for rides to the coast in my father's car or up into the Dales. We had our favourite haunts so to speak, usually pubs and overall had quite a sociable time. It was during this time both Walter and I were quite surprised to come across Eileen Ramsbottom in one of our more respectable haunts. Surprised we were because from knowing her at school, a pub was the last place you would have expected to find Eileen but there again I had changed and she had certainly filled out nicely. As you might expect she wasn't on her own. Her escort seemed a decent looking chap and lads being lads we weren't going anywhere until we got the 'low down' on him. He was called Graham and seemed to be a genuinely nice bloke and soon afterwards there were several occasions when we all enjoyed good evenings together. Graham hailed from the outer reaches of Leicestershire and they'd been courting for a few months now but more to the point, both he and Eileen wanted to get married. All of this seemed pretty sound stuff because he had a fairly decent job to do with the printing trade. That's probably why he was fairly clued up on some things. I think we were all a little surprised though, when during one of our social evenings at the local when he showed distinct concern as he told us Germany had invaded Czechoslovakia and more so as he informed us Britain had agreed to protect Poland. Germany wanted to invade Poland next. As he was a prospective husband I tried to appreciate his point of view but weddings and politics seemed rather heady stuff at this time. I must give the chap his due though, it gave us all food for thought which lasted well into the second pint. A couple of weeks later though, I knew I now shared his concerns as I took notice of Mousollini's Italian activities in Albania but as little seemed to be happening in or around Britain let alone Swinton, my usual interests preoccupied me. The only exception a couple of months later was the wedding of Graham and Eileen on 2 September. Although I was now good friends with both of them, the idea of attending their wedding did not appeal, but they both understood and I was delighted that they accepted my offer to take them to their new home in Leicester.

'Steady on Kenny, we're nearly there. Look there it is the one with the green door.' Even I could tell Eileen was proudly excited. And neither of them had complained on the journey down with being squashed in-between boxes and a couple of suitcases which can not have been comfortable and we must have been 2½ hours.

'Here you are Walter, go on and open up. You must come in and have a cuppa with us Kenny.'

'Of course, I'd love to.' So with suitcases and boxes more full of nick knacks than clothes and useful things, in we trundled after Graham. The house was very sparsely furnished a 'two up, two down' but this was their first day of marriage and their first home. It took a full fifteen minutes of delving into boxes and bundles to get the tea going on the old gas cooker but this was far more than compensated for by Walter demonstrating his new radio to me. He finally helped

Eileen in with the tea. They had enjoyed a small but lovely wedding yesterday and I had enjoyed a pleasant trip down with them today although I didn't let on I hadn't driven this far before! The radio had not been on five minutes and we were all relaxing and feeling quite pleased with ourselves when the programme was interrupted. Neville Chamberlain came on with a short austere speech telling the British public that as he hadn't heard from the Vice Chancellor of Germany about withdrawing from Poland, we were now at war with Germany. Only the radio was heard before Walter turned it off. The happy proud mood had been instantly transformed. God knows what they were thinking but this was really serious and I was annoyed as well. Out of so much doom and gloom, these two good folk, married yesterday on honeymoon today, get told as a wedding present that their country is now at war. I felt bad about it for myself but these two were on the only crest they'd be likely to get and even that was to be undermined by all the anxieties you could expect. On the one hand I was really pleased for them, for the wedding and moving to their new home but on the other hand it seemed a cruel sword of venom had touched their souls to taint any opportunity of their new life together. I couldn't do anything about their souls so in the absence of any other solution, we made light of it.

'Graham, Eileen,' I said, 'just twenty-odd years ago Germany was annihilated! They're just flexing their muscles.'

Then Eileen said with such venom 'Well you know what you can do with Mr. bloody Chamberlain then. Don't you?'

I had to agree but added 'They've taken Czechoslovakia but we've got the Empire behind us. They just need putting in their place. I bet it'll be all over by Christmas.'

'Kenny, you can't imagine how much I hope you're right.' We all knew this was a very optimistic outlook.

I made some rather poor cheerful conversation for a short while before I wished them all the best and bid my farewell. They came out on to the footpath to see me off.

'Kenny thanks ever so much. You bringing us here was a lovely present and it's helped us no end.'

'That's all right, Eileen. Just you make sure you look after yourself, and Graham.'

Looking directly at Graham I added, 'Alright?' He nodded 'and make sure you look after Eileen. Good luck.'

I wound the window up and was just making sure I engaged first without gnashing the gears as Eileen banged on the window.

'Remember. Keep due west for five or six miles then get on the A50 going north' she indicated to the sky overhead with her finger 'for Coalville and Burton-on-Trent.'

I nodded and gave her my impression of the fighter pilots 'thumbs up,' slipped the clutch and set off for the countryside. I had at least a two hour drive back and suddenly an awful lot to think about. Most Sunday afternoons were fairly quiet and although the road to Coalville was hilly it was pretty good and I made good progress. I was really pleased the car was going well because I was still annoyed with the news of the war spoiling the honeymoon of such a nice couple but to be more realistic, it was going to spoil a lot of other people's lives as well. I mean, who does he think he is? Germany is a lot bigger than Britain to start with. Hitler's already taken the Rhineland now he's taking Czechoslovakia AND Poland. Just how much does he want? And more to the point just how much is Chamberlain going to let him? What with Hitler and Mussolini in Albania wherever that is, things are getting really out of hand. I make no wonder we've declared war. Someone's got to put a stop to it. But where will the army go first? Germany, Poland, Italy? We're going to need loads of troops to sort this out. My realisation was that everyone will be needed to do his duty and this included me. I decided I'd just have to join up. Another mate of mine had joined the Ardwick Machine Gun Corps, a few months earlier and he said that it was alright. I knew the British Army was impressive and formidable but I didn't know much else about it.

I did know I was on a steep gradient as I had to change down a gear and at the same time had a flash of panic as I remembered I hadn't checked the water level before setting off as I also noticed the temperature gauge was much nearer the 'high' than it usually was. Fortunately the incline eased off and normal progress was resumed. And so did my annoyance with bloody Hitler. I didn't have a clue what options there were in the Army but I was certain I'd join what ever was shooting the bastards.

I was glad to approach Ashby-de-la-Zouch as the roads get quite hilly and twisty at times and I had to concentrate on my driving but once clear of the town it was a nice steady drive to Macclesfield. Any other time I would have loved it but today, there was just too much to take onboard. The truth is the only part of that section I remember is when it first hit the tram lines at the tram terminus on the outskirts of Macclesfield which sharpened my attention instantly! I got back home in the afternoon in quite good condition really. I think I must have talked myself round just about every angle there was on the situation and the only things I was sure of was that I'd go into Manchester and join up tomorrow, check the car over right now and have a drink with Walter this evening and see what he thought about it.

Manchester centre was never developed with the idea of accommodating parked vehicles and with the proverbial 'call to arms' radio broadcast yesterday there seemed to be every potential soldier and his brother milling around Princess Street either looking for the enlistment stations or forming queues outside them. I'd guessed it would probably be like this so I was quite pleased with myself that I'd gone on the 250cc Matchless. It was going well and looked OK and the thought of a crowd of people to witness my own impressive arrival was not totally unappealing. With the crack of the exhaust note as I gave it the final 'blip' of the throttle before killing the engine, right outside Garnhams as well, which was now the army enlistment station. I didn't think the queue of about twenty-five lads outside was too bad so I removed my goggles, turned my cap back round and waited my turn. After about ten minutes many more lads had joined the queue but I had moved up to be inside the shop that had been commissioned for enlistment services but I was then really daunted to see at least forty more enthusiastic souls patiently queuing inside to commit life and soul for their country. There was a right old cross section of folk from the rather sheepish looking quiet ones that were definitely going to join up but seemed very uneasy about it to the two 'loud-mouth' smart arses who were telling each other quite noisily and therefore everybody else where they were going to go, what they were going to do and how they were going to do it. That was until the smartly dressed one was called to the desk.

'Name and address?'

'John Kershaw. 164 Main Street Thornton'.

'Age?' asked the Sergeant looking rather bored. 'Eighteen' was the reply.

'Eighteen, what?' asked the Sergeant, in a somewhat curt manner.

'Eighteen and three months.' The lad replied, smiling.

This remark incurred something of a wry grin on the Sergeant and became the focus of attention for everyone else. 'Smiler,' the Sergeant started off, fairly quietly, 'take a bit of sound advice. If you want to see anything of the armed forces let alone tomorrow, you'd better start with recognizing the relevance of these'. He pointed at the three stripes on his arm. The lad wasn't really smiling now.

'Right. Placements. All armourment placings have been filled. We've got Motor Transport, Catering and Ordinance Disposal still open.'

'But I want to join the Tank Corps, my dad said I should.'

'Smiler!' the Sergeant said quite loudly. 'Do you need glasses? Do I look or even sound like your father? The answer is 'No Sergeant.' Is that clear?' The Sergeant was very loud now and the very subdued lad quietly repeated 'No Sergeant.' in acknowledgement.

'Let's continue, Motor Transport, Catering or Ordinance Disposal.'

'Motor Transport, Sergeant,' was the single reply.

'Sign your name there!' The lad signed. 'NEXT!'

Although they were more or less next to me, the queue went further in to the shop before doubling back to the desk. It sounded pretty clear to me I wasn't going to get into the Ardwick Machine Gun Corps in here and I was certain I wasn't going to be a cook or be a target for the enemy as an MT driver and I certainly wasn't going to try and blow myself up in the Bomb Disposal. I knew I'd have to do something else. To a silent chorus of abhorrent looks, I walked out of the shop. I had a slow walk and a cigarette to consider what to do. I was just meandering along and looking around when saw 'Walkers' shop occupied as the Royal Air Force enlistment centre. Got to be worth a look, I suppose.

I entered the shop and found the serving counter looking more like a desk top. 'Morning, son. Have you come to volunteer your services for King and Country?' a very alert chap in blue asked me.' Yes, really,' I answered 'but I'd like to know what job I'm signing up for' I added quite deliberately.

'Oh, that's easy' he said, 'What do you want to do?' This seemed remarkably civil to me. Looks like I'd done the right thing. 'Well I was going to join the Ardwick Machine Gun Corps but they're not taking anybody.'

'Right,' he said quite brightening up. 'So you want to see a bit of action do you?'

'You bet I do. Somebody's got to put Hitler in his place.'

'Good lad.' I noticed him look at my goggles and gloves. 'Are you on your motorbike?'

'Yeah, a Matchless 250cc.'

'Nice' he said.

'I used to have a 350cc Raleigh.'

'Do you fix it yourself?' I nodded.

'Good at mechanics and stuff.'?

'Yeah, sure.'

'And you want to give Hitler a real headache?'

'I sure do.'

'What's you name son?'

'Kenny, Kenny Butterworth.' With only the slightest of pauses I added 'Sergeant.' He couldn't help himself as half a smile appeared.

'Well Kenny, I've got just the job for you.' I still wasn't convinced but it all sounded promising.

'You'll work with machine guns and cannons on all sorts of aircraft, repair them and install them, learn about explosives and bombs and gun turrets. And you'll be able to put your name on as many bombs as you like and send them off to Hitler!'

Well it all sounded pretty good stuff. I was nodding in agreement.

'You'll be an Armourer in the Royal Air Force.'

'It sounds alright.' I then paused, but only just. 'I'll do it.'

'Right. These are your attestation papers. Sign, there. Lets have your full name and address and in a few weeks you'll get a letter of confirmation with details of your training unit and a travel warrant.

Well done.'

I walked out of the shop feeling really quite pleased with myself. I couldn't go back to work on the Hippo, fuel tanker, as it was half way through the round of deliveries, so resigned myself to enjoying an afternoon off and thought I'd chat with my mate Walter that night.

'What?' That was Walters's first reaction. 'You said you'd join the Ardwick Machine Gun Corps!' I was dealing with a rather irate Walter.

'Walter. I know I did. I was going to. I was in Garnhams but all the armourment sections were full.'

'So why'd you join the RAF?'

"Cos I wasn't going to be a driver or a cook. I'm going to be an Armourer in the RAF.'

'Well, I see what you mean. Looks like I won't see so much of you then.'

'Aw, c'mon Walter. The Sergeant said it'll be weeks yet, and we'll both have leave and stuff after that. You'll see.'

'Yeah, I suppose so.'

The following week, at work seemed surprisingly normal. Almost normal, apart from my partner, Dennis on The Hippo, trying to wind me up about the military. The weekend came round and although it wasn't a regular thing, I often did have tea on Saturday or Sunday with mum and dad, sometimes Walter came as well. This time I was on my own, though. When I went round to theirs, Mum was in the kitchen doing some sandwiches and sorting some pie out and dad was in the front room with his paper and the wireless. I did mum first.

'Oh my goodness. What on earth will you be doing?' then after a slight pause she turned to me 'And where will they be sending you? We might not see you for months!' She stepped toward me and gave me a hug. 'You might be a grown lad but you'll always be my little boy.'

Anyone might have thought that I'd just told her I was going to get the plague or something.

'Mum, it'll be alright. Don't worry.' Then she looked more serious than I ever remember.

'Kenneth' she addressed me. 'You weren't around twenty-two years ago, but I remember the last time.' I knew she was referring to the Great War, the war to end all wars! 'I know full well what I need to worry about.' Then I got another hug. She released me and shouted through to my dad 'Peter! Have you heard what he's gone and done?' With no reply she nodded to me to go through and tell my dad. I went through and he turned the volume down.

'What you got to tell me?' I told him I had enlisted in the Royal Air Force as an Armourer. 'What happened to the machine gun corps?'

'There were no places right now.' 'Well if you don't blow yourself up and keep your head down, we might just see you again then!'

'I guess that's about it' I said. He put his paper down and his glasses to one side and stood up, only slightly taller than myself. He stepped toward me and put a very strong arm around me with an equally firm grip and said quietly 'For God's sake Kenny, just tell me you'll think what you're doing?'

'Yeah, course I will dad.'

'And don't forget where your home is!'

As I didn't really know much about the forces or joining up, there wasn't much more to be said about the subject and general conversation followed. After a period of listening to the wireless after tea, my dad seemed to have a surge of enthusiasm. 'Come on mother. Let's get that piano warmed up!' and that was the start of one of their quite frequent musical soirees. I thought I'd grown out of them but I suppose recent events instilled both mum and dad to bring me 'into the fold' just one more time and doubtless it was not coincidental that the repertoire was particularly rousing! I went for a drink on the way back before turning in. The following weeks seemed quite normal really. The newspapers and billboards were telling everyone how serious the situation was but I was still delivering petrol for Isherwoods and still living at Walters and still seeing mum and dad at weekends. Even the fact that petrol rationing had now been introduced it still didn't really dampen things, probably because I didn't really know how much I used. Things really did seem quite normal. For four weeks, that's how life remained, until the most unobtrusive event started the countdown. I received my joining up papers.

CHAPTER TWO

Basic Training

There it was in black and white, I was now an Aircraftman Second Class engaged as an Aircraft hand/Armourer with a Draft No. 972694 and about to join No. 3 Recruitment Centre at Royal Air Force Padgate. The date was 14 November 1939. After reading the essential bits there were only two key questions to answer, one, where on earth is RAF Padgate and two, exactly how many weeks have I got left. When I found Padgate was only about twenty-five to thirty miles away I was actually a bit disappointed it wasn't further afield but overall, farther or nearer, it wasn't going to make a lot of difference. I can't honestly say I wanted to go to war but the idea of doing something different and even maybe going abroad was quite appealing.

So it was, with events as they were that I found myself waiting with a small suitcase and having to get a bus to the centre of Manchester. A bus of all things. I think the last time I caught a bus mother had to take me to the doctors. After the freedom of going everywhere and anywhere on the 250, it seemed one hell of a bind and even more so, having to walk across to Central Station. I didn't feel excited or that pleasure was imminent. I think it was a kind of feeling you get when you know you are entering the unknown. Nothing that you can be sure of, just one based more on hope, mainly that what wasn't going to be too bad. As I approached the station, to anyone's eyes, I was one of those going proudly, ready and willing to do my bit for King and Country. Once I was through the barrier and on the 'west' platform it became quite obvious who my other compatriots were. Even amongst the bustle of so many types of people, holding a single bag, looking uneasy, aged about eighteen to twenty years and uncomfortably dressed and mostly on their own apart from two of them who seemed to have brought half of their family, my imminent associates were clear. The station was a truly impressive place with a single huge great curved roof that spanned all the platforms and the hundreds of people that were milling about either leaving or arriving or were part of the army of handlers, porters and carriers that were shifting hundreds of pieces of luggage and freight all over the place. All the sounds of the bangings and knockings of trolleys and trains shunting back and forth and the broadcast messages reverberated around the great expanse of the station. Amazingly, all of these sounds were penetrated by one of the most obscure bellowing calls I had yet experienced. I was sure it was human but I couldn't tell what it was saying. Like so many other people I was looking round in earnest for where it came from. A few moments later it was repeated a 'something... something... something... Here.' On the 'Here' part I located the source, a solitary yet immaculate figure in RAF uniform with a very obvious clipboard at the ready. It didn't take any brains to recognise I needed to be where he was. With no more ado I and so many others made our way towards him. When he seemed to have accrued an acceptable number we had our first order.

'RAF personnel for Number Three Recruitment Centre over HERE. Form TWO lines.'

After about five minutes, he instructed us to 'pay attention.' In a very loud voice he addressed us.

'These two stripes on my arm,' as he pointed to them, 'tell you that I am a Corporal. When you hear your name, you will answer Yes Corporal. Is that **CLEAR**?' There was a collective murmur of an answer. Soon afterwards we boarded the carriage and were counted into each compartment. Conversation was a bit minimal as we each weighed each other up but I think most of us were from the Manchester area. It was a bit better when we felt the first jolt of the carriage as the engine took up the load and we were now on our way. The other lads seemed alright but I didn't hear anything that was interesting so I got drawn to the changing scenery through the window watching the countryside of Lancashire open up before me. It was years since I last sat watching so many different things going on through a train window. The only times I could remember, apart from a few day trips, was going on holidays with mum, dad and Llewellyn my brother. It was always Llewellyn that had to let me sit next to the window as he was three years my senior. I think the last holiday we had together was to north Devon but we had been to Wales and a place in Somerset as well. There is very little interesting about the countryside in November and I fought off the idea I was to be deprived of it for the next six weeks and I was brought back to the present company to establish my name and where I was from as the other lads were now making conversation. Pretty quickly I identified a few others that might have something in common with me. But at the moment we all had the same credentials, namely, young men, travelling alone, all with some form of well packed luggage and above all, none of us looking too bright about our future. The realization that others had taken similar steps to me was of some consolation, but not much, though I did feel a bit easier about it.

After about an hour and a painfully slow journey, our stop arrived and we were told most clearly to get off. There we were, all stood in a group on the platform, all looking around like rabbits just emerged from their burrow, myself included, trying to get our bearings. As a group we were directed to the barrier and once past the ticket collector, there was no doubt about it. 'Come on you lot, look lively.'

An RAF driver was stood casually on guard with his clip board, looking as though he wished he were somewhere else. He smartened up a bit when our corporal approached him. They spoke briefly, exchanged signatures then our corporal departed.

'All right, wait here. There's supposed to be fifteen of you, where the heck's the other two?'

How should I know, or the others come to that. Two minutes ago we had been thirteen individuals, suddenly not only were we a group but also responsible for two blokes we'd never seen.

'They're not going to like this. I was three short from the 10.15 am.' With that and a frown on his face, we were directed outside to our transport. There I had my first view of what was to become a most familiar sight. The rear end of a Bedford three tonner.

Duly arriving through the main gates of RAF Padgate, the driver stopped at the Guard Room and checked in his 'load' then continued into the main camp where we disembarked at a section for arrivals. After a brief glance around, I realized the place was totally in keeping with the weather at the time, cold, bleak and downright miserable, but only the weather might improve.

After ages of queuing, grouping and quoting of service numbers about a dozen times, we all ended up with an armful of kit and a billet number. After a group of us had traipsed across the camp to our billet, there we met the other half of our entry, so we numbered about fifty, in all. The only addition to uniform, boots, belt and bedding that we'd

BASIC TRAINING

been issued with was our 'dog tags,' one green, one red fibre. I was a little apprehensive about the reason why we were given two. I was told the red one, on a smaller loop was the one that got pulled off in the case of death or serious injury. That itself brought about a virtual competition by the lads in the room of who had heard or got the most macabre stories. Fortunately that was interrupted by a most significant arrival of our 'block' Corporal.

'Right you lot. Now you've enjoyed a little bit of 'R and R,' it's time to get settled in here. You've all got your uniform and a bed space. It is now 12.15 pm. I am going to return here at 1.30 pm. In the intervening period you will unpack your things, dress in your uniform, make your bed to the regulation standard, THEN, have lunch in the Junior Mess and report back here BEFORE 1.30 pm. If there are no questions, I'll take it you all understand what you have to do.' He remained paused for a moment then turned and went out. Then all the commotion started. Everyone was quizzing everyone else about what they had got, what it was called and how they should wear it and it was truly amazing just how many lads had no idea how to make a bed. The Corporal was going to have a field day later on. Out of what must have been a few hundred blokes there, I never would have thought they all fitted either a small medium or large, whatever it was. We had the impression we were been given an hour and a quarter to do a few simple tasks. It was just chaos, for exactly an hour and a quarter.

Amazingly our entry managed to become assembled as a recognizable group on the main square which must have covered acres. Even out in the open though you could not escape the smell of mothballs and to stand still was nigh on impossible as the new crisp blue serge started to abrade our unaccustomed skin.

At first, our attention was attracted to a couple of other entries practising drill. The way so many men moved so precisely together quite impressed me AND they wore their uniforms correctly. Something I was sure would be put right with us very soon. To find myself in the midst of so many RAF personnel almost instilled me with desire to get stuck in and become one of them as soon as possible. But then our Sergeant addressed us and it dawned on me and everyone else that from 5.30 am in the morning to 8.00 pm, the only thing I would be instilled with is the desire to get the job in hand done, sit down whenever I could and salute anything that looked like an Officer. It seemed like we were only to have cross-country running with Drill training before and after, Drill training and P.T. with Drill training before and after with only a couple of 'sit down' lectures during the week with Drill training before and after. So for the first fifteen minutes, I had been impressed by the RAF but then as I was progressively enlightened, I began to appreciate the fact that after six weeks it would all be behind me. In such a miserable place it was a dear thought that I desperately clung on to for five very hard weeks. I must have 'bulled' boots and buttons for days in total and if I'd had a bob for every mile we had marched, I'd swear I could have retired. But that wouldn't have done me much good because the amount of effort and sweat produced in the gym was nigh on killing me. The sixth week was different though. In that week we were told we could march and present our kit to the required standard, as K.R.'s and the D.I. decreed, and there were other 'green' entries about, but above all it was Christmas. It was also the week I heard rumours our Christmas dinner was to be served up by the Officers. This was hard to imagine as for the last five weeks any even casual confrontation had been avoided wherever possible. So with this in mind and generally being on top of the situation, there is a limit even for the RAF as to how much various items can be 'bulled,' the last week passed pleasantly quickly. The culmination being, officially knocking off early and the Christmas dinner. It was anticipation really that caused the excitement as all of us were new and suddenly we had a total role reversal. Although decorations in the Mess were spartan to say the least, they were evident. Dinner was served by Officers that we hardly recognized at first, due to the absence of uniforms on their part. But I knew there would be quite a few diners more familiar with the Officers in the morning, due to several unorthodox requests that were made upon the 'waiters.' Personally, it was the best meal I could remember having for several months.

But overall though having thought about it very carefully, I can honestly say that excepting the Christmas dinner, the only good thing about RAF Padgate was the road out of it and past the Main Gate and for the last time. As we had all finished basic training, we had all been privileged (we were told so) to get four days leave before joining our respective units for trade training. After a couple of celebratory pints in the Station Arms, for my return to Manchester, I made my way to the Commercial Hotel. As I arrived there I was warmed with greetings from my family and enjoyed a very pleasant albeit belated Christmas. It did seem a bit peculiar though. Nearly everywhere seemed not so much smaller but rather more closed in. Being in such familiar surroundings that formed an earlier age, I found myself almost surprised at commanding such respectful interest from my mum and dad who had so often previously been needed to sort Llewellyn and me out and keep an eye on us. Like when I was caught having an underage drink with him through meeting my friends on the bikes, to having a run out with other friends in our car. For all that had been miserable at Padgate, I had at least got used to the openness of the barrack and training blocks and the layout of the camp. The following day I visited Walters's family with seasonal greetings. To cover my humbleness at having to collect my remaining possessions, I assured them the RAF would take good care of me and besides, they could well use the space.

Having only one free day left as I had to travel to my next Unit the day after, the time just disappeared. Those four days leave over Christmas seemed to go like so many hours.

It was only over those few days of leave I found out just how strongly the Germans were advancing. In training all our time had been taken up with the stuff we had to get though, leaving any details of the German advance open to speculation and hearsay. Everyone had a pretty good idea of the Germans progress, but nobody wanted to believe it was so rapid in reality. I think it was because things were so quiet that it seemed at times so many people weren't interested in the war and just putting on a brave front, pleasantly talking about anything else, but the truth of the matter was Britain's general situation wasn't looking very good at all.

CHAPTER THREE
An Armourer

After leaving Manchester Central on the 8.42 I managed to join No. 2 Air Armourment School at RAF Pembrey on 30 December with only one change of trains. It was only when I was nearly there I realised I felt completely different to when I was joining my other station for the first time. I was a proper Airmen in uniform now and although I hadn't been to my destination before, I had a pretty good idea of what I'd find there when I arrived. I knew I wouldn't have drill practice every day, I knew I wouldn't have P.T. three times a week or kit inspection twice a week and thank goodness I knew I wouldn't have to get up at 0530 hrs in the morning six days a week. After the amount of 'bull' we had all experienced almost any situation was an exciting prospect. None of that now. I was going to learn about munitions, firearms, explosives, aircraft weapons and bombs. I was going to be part of giving the old krauts quite a headache. By the time the train pulled into Pembrey I had got the Third Reich bottled up with a handful of pilots and a dozen armourers. But knocking someone's case off the luggage rack, squeezing past a rather large woman in the corridor and wrestling with a reluctant carriage door quickly brought me down to earth as I got off the train. Once past the ticket collector and through the station there was the familiar 'back end' of the 3 tonner for the final leg to RAF Pembrey.

On arrival it was evident it was a newly built station as the Station HQ, the guardroom and the a few other buildings were brick built, there were several Nissen huts and the eighteen man billets were wooden.

Although Padgate had been a miserable place I thought, at least our billets had kept the weather out, which in the middle of winter they damn well needed to.

We went through the arrival procedure at SHQ where we also received our respective training locations, reporting times and billet numbers. It was only on the way to the billet that I got a little bit sick.

1. Locations in United Kingdom

For the whole journey here, I'd managed to keep my near gleaming boots virtually unmarked. The same boots I'd bulled up for the last five weeks. Now, in the last 200 yds they were ruined with mud and earth up to the ankles. I entered the billet taking care that at least the mud was off the soles, after a brief conversation with a few of the occupants I found my bed number and unloaded my kit. It must have been a bit obvious I was pondering how best to clean my boots up.

'Come in the front way did you?'

'Yeah.'

'You should've gone round the side. It's grass, but it's not boggy.'

'Thanks.'

'Never mind, they're nowhere near so keen on that sort of thing round here.'

From this brief exchange I quickly realised this chap was from a similar part of the country to myself.

'Do you know Manchester then?'

'Of course I do.'

'Princess Street?' I said grinning. A nod with a reluctant smile acknowledged.

'Still we're here now,' he said. 'Come on, we've got time to go to the Naafi before reporting.' As an afterthought, he added 'I'm Jack.'

'Hi, I'm Kenny.'

All our entry were training to be armourers, there was about forty of us housed in two billets, but as individuals we were a very mixed bag from all over the country. As such, there were all types of personal kit strewn in and around the bed spaces, a total contrast to Basic Training where everything had to be packed away and inspected as well, leaving sod all room for any personal stuff. Straight after some lunch in the mess, which impressed me immediately as the food was so much better, we were all seated in a very cold classroom being given our first lecture to be armourers. Being fairly mechanical minded, I felt quite comfortable learning about various weapons and how they worked, well I did at first. After a couple of days I realised that with the number of machine guns, rifles and revolvers that were involved, not to mention the different types of bombs like General Purpose, Armour Piercing 2,000 lb.ers and semi-Armour piercing 1,000 lb.ers with their detonators and fuses and the 'camera gun,' there might be a bit more to it than I first thought. All of them had different rates of fire, different components and ammunition, all of which had to be duly learnt and drawn up. We had to learn how to use hand tools and make simple components. Something Walter Briggs had wished I'd learned a bit earlier, before I'd joined up. At one time I'd made a new number plate for my bike and not 'quite' finished it off as the corners were left with sharp edges. Walter Briggs found out just how sharp they were when I set off a bit quick and he slipped off the pillion seat and caught the inside of his leg on the sharp corner. It was rather nasty.

One of the tools everyone was a bit nervous of was the clearing rod which was an inauspicious rod about five feet long with one end hollowed out. They were rarely used but when needed they had to be used correctly otherwise the results could be fatal. By and large all ammunition was made to very exacting standards but sometimes cartridges were made incorrectly, sometimes individual cartridges got damaged making them out of shape and sometimes incorrect ammunition might be used in a gun. In all these cases, when the cartridge was pushed into the breech of the gun barrel it got stuck. Whether a cartridge was lightly stuck or stuck really tight, to remove it involved the use of the clearing rod. The hollow end was inserted into the barrel to engage with the nose cap of the cartridge that was stuck. The pneumatic cocking lever was operated from the cockpit whilst a lever on the gun was pulled. The force used was then increased to dislodge the cartridge in question. If it was really tight the rod was slid down the barrel with greater force but in these instances there was always some possibility of the shell exploding in which case the rod would exit the barrel at about 150 mph, therefore the final instruction was always 'ram the rod and duck.'

Later on we covered hydraulics and principles of operation of aircraft gun turrets. The gun turret was interesting because we were lucky enough to have a real working example to study all set up in a dome like brick building. Apart from the guns used in training, it was a large piece of real hardware we could expect to come across on real aircraft. All in all we were kept busy with lots of practical dismantling and assembly, but it was at least interesting as well. On one occasion I was taken back a few years earlier to when I was fourteen years old at home, just after dad was out of hospital and just before I left school. I was getting a little more cocky with looking after the car and having 'built' our garage, so I decided to give our old Cowley a de-coke. I took the cylinder head off (side valve) and cleaned it up alright; I even reassembled it with only a small amount of advice and got it running again, very much to my relief. When it was running though, I started having my doubts when I realised the bulk of the exhaust smoke was steam. Something was leaking inside the engine, quite probably, the head itself. With much consternation from Llewellyn, the car was put 'in dock.' As it happened, not long afterwards dad came home. It amazed me how well he took the 'news,' I knew he was well displeased though, but he took it to the garage where the head was removed, a new gasket fitted and then put back together. It was fine.

Out of a room of about twenty blokes it was natural that several circles of friends were established that all of us drifted into, be it for companionship or out of common interests. The only exceptions were a couple of academic type 'swots' who didn't really mix and always seemed to be reading. Then there was Duffy, a quiet chap who always seemed to be scruffy. It turned out he was a bit 'thick' really and we all found out it was pretty difficult to insult him. He always latched on to which ever group was most tolerant of him at the time. I felt sorry for him sometimes, but that's all. I was fortunate that Jack Pritchard had the next bed to mine. We had quite similar backgrounds and got on really well. It was slightly puzzling for both of us that out of all the different service numbers used, his number was 972695 and mine was 972694. Before joining up he had been involved with printing machinery.

Not all the tedium of basic training was escaped as we still had cross country running one afternoon per week. Although something of an effort, it was a pleasant change from being in the class room all week, when it wasn't freezing or raining, to which the P.T.I.'s seemed quite immune. It went without saying that the camp was new because it wasn't even finished and this was probably why all the classrooms were unheated, a fact that apparently warranted an extra visit each day by the Naafi van. This was a small price to pay for the improved standard of food served in the mess compared to what we had been used to especially as food rationing was introduced on 8 January. What with free time in the evenings, decent food and not exactly been over worked, service life was taking a turn for the better.

At this time there was a general tendency, a sort of unofficial 'push' for service personnel to mix and be accepted more by the local community. I supposed it was in the interests of the general war effort, but either way, on the whole it seemed a good idea and therefore myself and Jack came into contact with a family at Llanelly.

Both Jack and I found them very friendly and it was a big bonus having conducive people in the locality to pass an afternoon with. They had a terraced house on the outskirts with two young children. Dick was a miner and Audwine, his wife. After the basics of RAF life it was just so pleasant to have tea in armchairs on a carpet and study the various ornaments on the mantelpiece. They were quite ordinary folk and both of us became quite friendly with them. It was after the first of the occasional Church Parades our intake had to do when they invited us for Sunday lunch after which we would sociably pass the afternoon with them. Before long we stayed for tea as well. I remember being a little apprehensive about accepting their offer to accompany them to Evensong but knowing Dick, I followed his suggestive wink that I should do so. Fraternising to this extent proved a little beyond Jacks expectations and politely he returned to camp. To the uninitiated it would be something of a daunting thought knowing only too well that pubs in Wales didn't open on Sundays and the only 'pint' to be had was on camp. But what it is to have faith! Being very regular people, Dick and Audwine's custom was to call in the 'social club' afterwards where all the wrongs of the previous week and the service were put to rights, if not at least agreed upon. All over a few pints just to be sociable! Although such pleasant familiarity was most welcome there was some price to pay for it. It came in the form of Dick's sister Ruby.

I never really knew just what to make of her; both Jack and I met her when she visited. She was a very pleasant woman, only a few years older but reasonably attractive, confident and casual but quite conscious of herself. She always seemed to visit on the same day Jack and I did, which could have been coincidence as it was at weekends but maybe not. Maybe she thought we were different or just liked our company but talked with us like an interested relation might but always with a twinkle in her eye and that's when she really looked attractive. Ruby really was a good conversation maker, not prattling on about all and sundry like you might expect. You could never reply yes or no as she had a rare quality of drawing people into conversation so Jack or I always had to explain our particular views or opinions. The fact she had her own Morris 8 told me quite a bit, enough I think, for her to remain a good friendly acquaintance. Even so, after a short while it developed into an exciting gamble as to whether or not we would be offered a lift back to camp.

The classrooms were always cold, but just once things did warm up a little. We were sat there, well buttoned up and hoping for an early arrival of the Naafi van, being instructed in the make up of detonators, bombs and Amatol and Baratol, high explosive. Suddenly as if from nowhere a rescue tender and another truck went racing past the windows being driven really hard. That was enough to interrupt the lesson but seconds later we heard a very low flying aircraft that sounded as if it wasn't flying very well at all. Those of us sitting anywhere near a window crowded up to them just in time to see a medium twin engined plane flying dead low with smoke coming from one engine. Remarkably everyone went silent, even the sergeant instructor. The silence held for many seconds while all of us 'listened' but on hearing nothing the instructor continued up till lunch time. The debate amongst the rest of us as to whether it landed or crashed, lasted right through lunch but I was to be the first one to know for sure.

First thing after lunch the sergeant addressed us in the classroom.

'Right, you lot that were sat by the window. Anybody recognise what aircraft it was?'

Aircraft recognition had been part of basic training and we all wanted to impress the instructor. Brightly, I raised my hand as well.

'Yes Butterworth?'

'An Anson Sergeant.'

'Well done lad. Ever been in one?'

'No Sergeant.'

'Well here's a prime opportunity for you. Go to the Guardroom and report to the Corporal I/C, you'll be able to make a detailed inspection of the aircraft.'

My moment of elation suddenly paled. After an extensive tour of the Welsh countryside, the hard way, my driver dropped me off at the crash site.

'Cor, it's a bit of a mess isn't it?'

'Yeah, just a bit.' I replied.

'I wonder how the crew are.'

'Well at best I reckon they had a fifty/fifty chance.'

'Anyway, I'll be off now. I'll be back with your replacement later on, see you.'

With that the driver turned the truck around and set off back across the countryside. Watching him disappear, I realised just how big the countryside was, how the weather was changeable and also dusk wasn't too far away. The Anson was wrecked with starboard wing and engine thirty yards away and all the front of the fuselage completely stoved in. My Sergeant had been right though, after a couple of hours I had inspected every part of that aeroplane. What else would I be doing, stuck out on a Welsh hillside. It was about 3 hours later, just as it was getting dark when my replacement arrived. From inside the plane I'd shot them up completely as they approached! It wasn't long before I found out exactly what had happened to the crew of three because they were accommodated in our billet for the night. It seems that it was a simple matter of a hydraulic valve failing, or the linkage that prevented the landing gear operating.

Jack Pritchard and I became good mates and virtually did the course together. There were several others we were both mates with but it was usually Jack that I walked the two miles to the village with for a pint or two. At that time of year, it was only at weekends we had any free time in daylight, but due to my luck or the lack of it, I had a temporary change. During the week we were walking down the lane to the village at night. There wasn't much traffic in the evenings. As usual we talked about all sorts and had no cause to notice a car approaching from behind as we casually walked at the edge. But it seemed that wasn't good enough for this driver who wanted a bit more room. My heart literally missed a beat as a large front wing smashed into my right side and leg, ejecting me instantly on to the grass verge where I saw stars that really danced around. I think I was 'out' for a few seconds as I only remember Jack shouting 'Kenny, Kenny are you alright?' A very nervous Jack as well. In the near darkness I was totally disorientated. Then I was with Jack. Then I was sick with pain. I felt Jacks hands finding my position. My arms seemed fairly safe to move but the right one hurt a lot. I tried my legs.

'For Christ's sake!' my first words as a searing pain shot up my right side.

'Mad bastard.' at least Jack knew I was conversant.

'Kenny, can you move?'

'How much?' I asked through clenched teeth.

'I don't know, anything.'

With much cursing I managed to get on to my left side where after a few minutes we established that nothing major was broken, but the pain was hell.

'We'll have to get you back.'

'Yeah, I'll go along with that.'

'Right.' There was a few moments pause as I knew Jack would be logically going through the alternatives that might be available. At the same time I was becoming a bit more collected as well.

'OK, I'll give you a piggy back. If someone comes along, we'll get a lift.'

It seemed a bit ambitious, but what else was there? Trying to catch up with his thoughts, I reckoned we were only about three quarters of a mile from camp as well. With considerable effort, we both compromised on an acceptable position and off we went. With only two stops, Jack carried me all the way to the camp. As we arrived at the guard room I couldn't say who was the most relieved, we were just glad to get there. The sum total was that I ended up in the medical centre for three days in tension with an awful lot of bruising and pulled ligaments. I was pleased Jack came to visit but I suspect a few of the other lads only came to see our Entries first casualty of the war, in the flesh so to speak. I was only kept in for three days but how boring it was. I was in training, in a strange place where I hardly knew anyone and couldn't do anything. It was a nice enough ward and I did see nurses now and again but they didn't stop long or say very much! I would have swopped all the niceties to be in a garage with a radio and a couple of magazines. But how I wished my old pal Walter Briggs would come through that door. There wouldn't be any chance of that though and having so much time on my hands only allowed myself to be further plagued with the thought of his death from three years ago. Walter Briggs had been another good friend of mine, and lived about

¾ mile from me. He had a similar motorbike and at the time we shared common interests namely cars, bikes and beer. We had many good times and rides together and sometimes raced between our various haunts. Sometimes we'd go around the countryside and the moors or to a club in Warrington that had tennis courts as well and sometimes we went to Blackpool. I always enjoyed going to Blackpool because being sixty miles away, there was always the challenge of 'doing it' in an hour. Sometimes we 'went for it' and sometimes we took our time but it was usually me that wanted to 'go' for the hour. The 'time trials' practice came to an abrupt end one morning. We were on a run out in the countryside with good roads, and nice sweeping bends. I was on the inside with Walter just in front and a little further out as we came to a slight rise with a left-hander at the crest. The weather was fine and we were both going well. It was like a momentary instant as one second he was there and the next, he had slid fully into the path of a 5 tonner coming up the other side and lost half of his head in the matrix type radiator. His bike lay in a bed of heather virtually undamaged. The instant change of feeling and shock will forever be in my mind as I realised the full consequences. The only consolation I had was although it was a messy end, it had been very quick. It was only then I heard for the first time a distant voice in the back of my brain. 'There but for the grace of God, go I.' His parents ran a newsagents and tobacconist shop. They never got over it.

After three days in 'dock,' even though my right side was still really sore, I was so bored I made sure I got discharged. As far as I could make out, the only good thing to come out of getting knocked over was a heaped double helping of sympathy from Dick's sister, which lasted the remaining four weeks of the course.

By the end of March, we had all passed the various tests of the course, including 'Duffy,' God help us, and on 28 March I received my first real posting to 50 Sqdn at RAF Waddington in Lincolnshire, just about the other side of the country. But I was an Armourer!

CHAPTER FOUR

First Posting

After the experience of Padgate and Pembrey, I felt distinctly optimistic about the prospect of going to RAF Waddington, like I used to feel when we went for summer holidays. I was high with confidence, satisfaction and expectation. To be part of the structure that was Britain's prime most force could not happen soon enough. Rather than the countryside being my idea of freedom being left behind, it was now my country, my sovereign country I was viewing, that I was going to defend. So it was with casual presumption, after leaving Lincoln station on 29 March, I boarded the three tonner for RAF Waddington.

'Hiya mate. What bed you got?' the sole occupant, a pleasant enough chap reclining on his bed greeted me as I entered the billet, obviously from London.

'Seventeen.'

'Over there, next to the one with the rucksack.'

'Thanks.' After officially arriving at the Station Headquarters this was my first stop late in the morning. It seemed a cheery enough place and I was glad to see the linoleum wasn't too glossy. There was a lot to be said for brick built billets.

'Did that corporal at SHQ give you any of that crap about reporting for duty immediately?'

'Yes he said something about that.'

'Well, it's up to you, but you might as well make the most of it here for an hour. By the way, I'm Joe.'

'Hi, Kenny.'

'Well Kenny, you are one of the 'heavies' now, 'ow about a pint in the mess, they're open shortly?'

'Sounds good to me.' and so it was that I met Joe Reader. He was an armourer on 50 Sqdn and quickly became a good mate of mine. He had fair hair, was a bit taller than me and was alright. We used to go for a drink together. The station seemed a nice place, as it was finished with good permanent barrack blocks and a NAAFI. That afternoon I met the others in the Armoury, most of who were in the same billet. With a couple of Sergeants and three Corporals we numbered about twenty in all. The sergeants were billeted in the sergeants' mess while corporals were generally put in charge of a dormitory in the airmen's billets, having their own personal room near the entrance. Depending on 'flying operations,' those who had been covering night duties were 'stood down' during the day. We worked in groups of four or five, but this varied with 'operational' requirements. I was to be with Frank, Joe Reader, Alan and Johnny Johnson. There was plenty of work which was interesting and worthwhile because 'it was to the detriment of the enemy.'

There was some training in the armoury but mostly it took place outside on the actual aircraft on 'the line.'

Today we were on 'the line' aircraft.

'Who are the two new lads Corp?'

A breathless airman addressed Frank, from astride his bicycle. Johnny and I was getting bomb winching familiarity. Stooping from under the aircraft into bright sunshine, a very narrow eyed Frank replied 'Butterworth and Johnson, why?'

'Serge wants them over the Armoury, pronto.'

'Alright.' With that the airman rode off with some degree of urgency.

'Well, what you two been up to?' As he spoke we got a sickening feeling.

'Nothing Corporal, honest.'

'Well, you'd better get yourselves over there, sharpish.'

It was Johnny's eighth and my third day at the station and neither of us could figure out what we had done wrong! As we arrived at the Armoury office a sergeant met us.

'You two, ah good. Get yourselves in the workshop. There's been a bit of an accident and it needs clearing up.'

We obeyed immediately as we were so relieved it wasn't anything to do with us.

'Well, it can't be too bad Johnny.'

'How do you make that out?'

'Well if there'd been a serious accident, I reckon that most of the armoury would be blown away.'

'Yeah, I suppose so.'

We walked past the benches seeing nothing out of the ordinary, at first that is. Then we saw blood on the floor, which led to a trail of blood. This in turn led to a bench where there seemed to be gallons of the stuff. It was all over the duck boards, the floor and the front of the bench behind.

'Hell fire Kenny. I think they've brought the war over here by the looks of this.' I was amazed really.

'Yeah.'

Even after gallons of hot soapy water and a couple of hours solid scrubbing it was cleared up alright but you could still see a stain wherever it had been.

I could see why it lasted so well in prehistoric cave drawings. It turned out some prat had shot himself through the groin whilst cleaning a .45 revolver. It was a good job he was in the medical centre because after that amount of toil for his stupidity, I could easily have given him another round! That evening, over a pint, Joe thought he was a stupid gyte as well.

Whatever good times were to be had in the evenings were made by ourselves but there wasn't an awful lot of scope on camp. This is where I was fortunate as after a couple of weeks I had managed to bring the Morris down. Technically we were on duty seven days a week but by taking a healthy interest in Operations, via the 'grape vine' it became quite easy to go out to one of the towns in the evenings, usually Lincoln but occasionally we went to Nottingham. Usually I changed into civvies so if we were checked at any time it would appear that I was off duty and thereby avoid any awkward questions.

It was about four weeks after my arrival that Joe and I were having a drink in a different pub in Nottingham that we'd been told about as it was supposed to be the oldest pub in England. It was called the Trip to Jerusalem and was located at the base of a sort of rock hill that Nottingham Castle was built on. We went in and got a couple of pints, I think it only seemed crowded because really it wasn't so large.

'There you are Joe,' I said. 'I told you it was really old. Look up there. The date is in that old wood beam.'

'Oh, yeah. Is that 1198?'

'Yeah, sure is.'

'Wow, I bet this place has seen a bit of action in its time.'

As it was a smallish pub, it wasn't packed out but there wasn't a lot of space either and different groups were easily within ear shot. After a couple of pints we decided to leave. As it was about 08:15 pm there was a steady general movement of people and we had no reason to notice a few 'well oiled' lads following us out. That is until we just got out of the pub. They must have been drunk, but they'd got some sort of mission on Joe. I still can't figure out why. Maybe it was something to do with him being in uniform and a 'southerner' and me in civvies and a 'northerner' or just mistaken identity. Come what may, they were gunning for Joe and went for him something rotten. It was all pretty quick but with five of them in the fray things happened pretty quickly. I wasn't going to stand for this and didn't have to think about helping him out and waded in to help him. They really didn't go for this as I think they thought I was one of 'them,' so they turned on me instead. They were kicking and punching me even when I was on the ground and as Joe had got a bit of a pasting, he'd gone off somewhere. I was getting really annoyed and decided I'd had enough of this. What wasn't obvious though was I had a .38 pistol with me, which I knew I shouldn't but this was a rather desperate situation. I got my pistol out and let off a round 'somewhere' upwards. It did go upwards but seriously parted someone's hair on the way! Then I belted another of them across the head with the pistol, which partially scalped him. After the shot and with two of them writhing in agony, the others ran off. As my luck would have it, by the time the police arrived, I was the only one left to arrest, which they proceeded to do as Joe had disappeared and the remaining two youths were seriously injured and it was my gun!

I was taken to the Police Station and charged with amongst other things, attempted murder! Using service ammunition, using service petrol, being in civilian dress in wartime, being more than twelve miles from camp and not being booked out. I got handed over to the RAF police to face a formal hearing. I was 'detained' in the guardroom for a couple of days while 'those in that position' prepared my 'hearing.' On the day I went before the Commanding Officer and told my story. When I had finished there were a few moments consultation then I was told by the CO.

'Things like that do not happen in this country!' Accept my punishment or face a Court Marshal.'

It made my stomach twist as I said 'your punishment.' I was awarded twenty-eight days in the 'glass house.'

Quite simply it was a terrible place. I was worked like a dog, the facilities were basic enough to be downright crude and I was chased around and shouted at from dawn till dusk doing all sorts of pointless 'work' and cleaning just about anything that was used. In that short period of time at the end of each day, before sleeping from exhaustion despite the cold, my outlook was radically altered. Unlike the majority of the inmates, I really had done nothing wrong. It was only because some tarted-up Wing Commander didn't know what the real world was like, that I was there. I remember thinking at the time, if this is the calibre of the commanders of our armed forces, it's no wonder Hitler is making such good progress.

I returned from my 'holiday' very much leaner but was very self conscious of my suspiciously short hair, even the new recruits had more hair than me but at least I'd look good on parade. As I was about to leave my 'holiday' camp, I was given my papers which included my travel warrant and details of my next posting. It was customary practice to post people away after any real trouble but for all the crap I had received, the slightest glimmer of reprieve came in the form of an internal posting to 44 Sqdn. I was staying at RAF Waddington!

I had resolved myself to the fact that although there may be some 'dickhead' at the top of the tree, by and large it was a nice camp and I liked it here.

But I was truly devastated as I found out why my relocation appeared to be such a trivial matter. My enlightenment came as I was formally 'arriving' at the SHQ at Movements where it seemed a good place to enquire about Joe.

'Aw, c'mon corp, He was my best mate. I only want to know where he went.' The movements Corporal seemed aghast to be asked of the whereabouts of one airman. I could tell by the way he hissed through his teeth and his face was screwed up that he felt pretty strongly about the matter. I still didn't think it was unreasonable though until he continued.

'Where the Hell have you been these last weeks? Been blind AND deaf? Eh?' I was now shaking my head in wonderment.

'Have you read any newspapers lately?'

'No.' I replied.

'What about news broadcasts, heard any of them?'

'No, Corporal.' He really was a bit wound up now, nearly lost for words.

'Ye gods, where on earth have you been lately?'

Sheepishly I said 'Away.'

'I just don't believe this. OK, it's like this.' He calmed down a little now.

'Hitler has given me a bit of a problem'. He paused. 'He has managed to push 350,000 of our troops on to the beaches of France.' His speech was more deliberate now.

'They have nothing to fight with and no rations. They have the Germans hammering them from the front and only the sea at their backs. Everyone is trying to evacuate them but they're getting shot up as I'm telling you this. I have to tell them upstairs just how many of those 350,000 can come here. And they want to know yesterday! Now for Christ's sake leave me alone and ask Sally over there.'

Without a word I turned away. I asked Sally, only to be told Joe had been posted abroad, but I couldn't find out where. Somehow they must have latched on to Joe being involved as well. I really could sympathise with the Corporal though. Having to evacuate all our troops from France was bad enough, but the thought of what it meant for Britain against Germany was just terrible.

Within a day or two some of those troops did arrive, and a sorry state they were in too. It made my time in the 'glass house' seem insignificant. These men had been weeks in the front line, all were battered, weary and hungry. Nearly all of them were in rags which doubled as bandages and stained in blood, mud and sand but they all thought they were the lucky ones. Those that didn't get back, were the unlucky ones. This episode was the result of 'Operation Dynamo,' the retreat of our expeditionary forces from France. After a few days I got to know a few of them, they all had the same appalling story. Being shot at and bombed day and night, no cover, nothing to shoot back with and only the sea at their heels.

Shortly afterwards I heard that invasion barges across the Channel for German troops had been bombed. The aircrew told me bodies were definitely being found for ages. Rumour was this had prevented a planned invasion of Britain. Either the Germans had lost a lot of troops and thought we were stronger than they expected or their intelligence had been breached. The truth was they didn't have air supremacy, yet.

CHAPTER FIVE

44 Squadron

As I was now with 44 Sqdn, I worked more on the aircraft on the hard standing and in the hangers rather than in the Armoury. Now I fell in with another group of lads that were alright but I was quite aware I needed to settle down a bit and get on with helping to win the war. In the period I'd been away it seemed Hitler had taken most of Europe by invading France, Belgium, Denmark and Norway. All within a few weeks! The squadron had been operating Hampdens for the last year and a half. They were a medium, twin engined bomber. Due to the narrow tail section they always reminded me of a giant black wasp. They did have a bit of a sting though with twin Vickers 'K' guns in both mid-upper and mid-lower gun turrets. The navigator occupied a Perspex dome in the nose with a single gun while the pilot was above and slightly rearward with a fixed Browning .303 (ring and bead sight) overhead on the port side.

I had a pretty good induction to the Hammies by Dave Cross. He was a Sergeant Armourer, but also an Air Gunner and Wireless Operator. It was so much easier to take things in from an Air Gunner that it was a pleasure to learn. He had flown lots of missions in action and as such, gave a really clear picture of what was needed, highlighting the smaller details that either made the job easier or better.

Our duties were either armoury based or as termed, Flight Duty, which was more interesting. When an aircrew were 'stood down,' daily inspections of various mechanisms had to be done including checking turrets and hydraulics, cleaning guns and testing bomb racks. It wasn't treated as routine either as at any time of the day or night these aircraft could be required to take off in action as soon as they could be loaded with the specified bomb type. As a result training took place as and when the opportunity arose. This was done in small groups of two or three so what we were being shown had to be taken in and got right. There was no time to get things wrong. The day I was on 'bombing up' Johnny Johnson was with me, he was alright and in the same billet. I was on the winch in the fuselage and he was guiding the bomb rack in from underneath. Unfortunately whilst 'bombing up,' both of us made a small mistake, much to Johnny's cost. Evidently he was checking the alignment of the rack in the fuselage by feeling with his finger that the holes lined up for the rod, but I winched up a bit early. It seems I sheared the end of his finger off. We both knew it was an accident and he said he wasn't angry but he really did grimace a lot! An ambulance was called and whisked Johnny away with his detached finger wrapped in brown paper off to Sick Quarters. That was the last I heard of him. There were always new faces appearing and more so now as in June the age of conscription was raised to forty-one years.

The missions of the squadron were usually carried out under the cover of night so as Operations instructions were received, the load for two or three aircraft at a time would be brought over in the afternoon or evening on trolleys from the Bomb Dump (store) then pre-armed to have the 'release' checked before being loaded. The work was usually finished around teatime, but how those controllers cursed when orders came through for a change of bomb type!

All the squadrons were made up of a number of Flights and the aircraft used to take off in ones and twos, circle the airfield then form up with usually about twelve or more to a Squadron. On bigger missions several Squadrons would form up together to form a 'Wing.' When aircraft returned from a mission we had to be on the tarmac to receive them. The pilot would open the bomb doors for us to check for unreleased bombs which might be held in the bomb doors, before they taxied to their relevant dispersal areas.

About a fortnight after my arrival with 44 Sqdn they took part in a raid on German warships. On 10 June 1941 about 40 Wellingtons of 38 Group, 28 Whitley's and about 40 Hampdens took off for a massed raid on the German warships *Scharnhor*st, *Gneisenau* and *Prinz Eugen* in the port of Brest. These ships were the pride of the German navy and fast becoming famous for their resilience to attack. The mission was successful but no permanent damage was done to the ships. I know all our Hampdens returned safely but didn't get told about the others. Another similar mission took place on 13 June but again no permanent damage was done.

Occasionally Dave Cross was on duty in the Armoury and as he was an Air Gunner/Wireless Operator I got on pretty well with him as I was interested in the radios. After a couple of weeks I became acquainted with a friend of his, Burt Hare, a Sergeant Air Gunner.

Rank was always respected, it had to be but where familiarity through work occurred, many friendships were formed throughout the services that bridged the difference of rank. With Burt, I found we had a common outlook on life and became good friends. Often I would go over to his billet and hear the latest news on his prized possession, a Philco 4 valve radio or just have a chat with him. One June evening Burt had been a bit quiet when he turned the radio off. He didn't seem himself. There weren't many options to address this problem but going for a drink usually worked.

'I was thinking of going to the Red Lion tonight, fancy a drink?'

'That's a good idea Kenny. I fancy a couple tonight.' This sounded OK but it wasn't said with his usual casualness.

'I thought Dave would be coming, he's stood down, isn't he?'

'Well that's it Kenny, Dave's been stood down for good.'

'What-what? What do you mean?' His manner and the way he said this did not make me feel very comfortable.

'I mean Kenny,' Burt paused, out of character. 'Dave has drunk his last pint and flown his last mission. He didn't make this one.' There was a long silence between us, a silent recognition of respect no words could create. This situation was all too common, but it was never easy either.

'Come on Kenny. Off to the Red Lion. We'll just have to drink Dave's for him.'

'Yeah, sure.'

As Waddington was an operational station, new faces were always arriving and although they had the trades that were required most of them hadn't worked on Hampdens before. For this reason Familiarization Programmes were essential for both aircrew and ground crew and a very important part was bombing practice. This took place in a more remote part of the airfield where 11 ½ lb smoke practice bombs were used for target practice on a marked out area. To record the accuracy, someone had to watch where the bombs fell, another of the armourers' duties. This was done from a hut on the peritrack which overlooked the quadrant site bomb area. The impact area was noted in relation to the target, then with a sextant and compasses the actual position of the burst was plotted on a grid map to give the margin of error.

When on this duty I often thought about Burt in action in the Hampdens. Instead of a sunny afternoon, Burt was in that Hammie, flying in the cold pitch darkness towards more blackness with the constant drone of the engines humming away. All too often flying towards a potential cauldron of searchlights and just waiting for the anti-aircraft flak to start up with the scores of lethal tracer lines weaving across the sky. Hoping that when the shrapnel was exploding all around he would be lucky enough for it to miss him. All this and still waiting for a shot at the defending night fighters. I was there supporting Burt and defending my country. It was me searching the night sky, desperately looking for the slightest glimpse of moonlight reflecting off a wing or maybe the flash of an engine exhaust or a distant burst of gunfire as a tell tale sign of the enemy. You had to be quick, you only had the trace of their first burst of cannon fire to take aim on. If they were unlucky, you may be lucky but luck was in short supply.

The bad luck side of things was brought home to me a bit more when I saw a Hammie crash on landing. After watching so many landings I was a pretty good judge of approach. On this particular afternoon, three Hammies were doing circuits of bombing practice and they had all done three or four circuits when one of them, on the final approach just came in too low. It was obvious that the engines prevented him from getting the nose up. He just made it on to the runway but the full load bounced down on the wheel struts which hesitated then sank into the fuselage allowing the body of the aircraft to pancake along the runway. The props just folded up as the engines and hydraulics were ripped apart amid great clouds of smoke and vapour which quickly ignited into flames as it came to a standstill by which time the hatches were already open with a very desperate crew scrambling out. Within seconds the flames had tracked back to the fuselage which became engulfed as the intense heat let the wings fold to the ground amid a thick black plume of smoke. All this happened in just a few seconds. The thought of the crash played on my mind for the rest of the day. After all, I'd been trained on the service and repair of aircraft and even though I'd studied the wreckage of the Anson, actually seeing the speed and intensity by which the heat and flames reduced the whole aircraft to a pile of twisted molten scrap metal made me have second thoughts for any aircrew, anywhere. I'm not sure why, but I just felt I really wanted to have a drink with Burt that evening, which I did.

After a couple of pints I had to tell him I'd watched the crash and felt brave enough to ask him about his job.

'Well you're not far off the mark there Kenny. It's a bit like riding motorbikes really. You know it's easy to fall off but you never think you will and you never think it will be bad.'

He drew long on his cigarette and I had the image of Walter impaled on the lorry before my eyes.

'It's the not knowing what you're going to get, or when, that's the problem. It's always a long ride but you can only scan the sights for so long, until you know it's essential.'

Suddenly he cheered up, like he'd just remembered something.

'Anyway Kenny enough talk of doom and gloom, eh? I didn't come here to talk about air crashes.'

We chatted a bit more but I could see he was leading up to something by talking about doing the right thing with families and stuff.

'See, it's like this Kenny. I've got to do something a bit important. I've got to get my mother something tomorrow or I'll never hear the end of it, but to do that I'll miss pay parade. Any chance that you could lend me 10s?'

'Yeah, sure Burt.'

'Thanks Kenny.' Then he paused. 'Look, it'll be a week or so before I can repay you. Just make me feel better and look after my radio, will you, until I do, OK?'

It was quite unnecessary, but that's what he wanted.

'Sure Burt, that's fine.'

After the fall of Dunkirk the mood of the whole station slowly but steadily became more serious. Nothing really obvious but there was far less casualness about people with more emphasis on manning levels and work loads. For the past month or more, bombing missions had been a regular occurrence but with Dave gone and the failure of our 2nd Expeditionary Force in France, the real plight of Britain was an increasing concern to everyone including me. A monumental moral blow was delivered whilst Burt and I was listening to the news in his room. The date was 18 July and only a small part of the broadcast etched itself on to my mind but that was enough, an extract of Winston Churchill's address to the nation. '...the battle of France is over. I expect the Battle for Britain is about to begin.'

A month later it did begin and in earnest. On 13 August alone, the Luftwaffe conducted 1,485 sorties over England knocking out our aircraft at a ratio of four to one. From there on, there were bombing raids nearly all the time mostly on the airfields down south but the sirens were sounded around Waddington a fair bit as well. The newspapers and broadcasts were full of the exploits of Fighter Command and the heroic efforts they were making as Britain's only significant protection was progressively eroded. The pilots had the admiration of everyone but unfortunately this was not enough. The odds were against them and as they were Britain's last line of defence, the odds were against Britain remaining a free island. This really was the battle for Britain.

The state of Fighter Command was a pretty dismal affair during this time as they were taking heavy losses on the ground as well as in the air. The airfields and runways were instantly patched and repaired every time by as much dedication and commitment that every man and woman could muster. But at least it left what there was of us bomber squadrons to do what we could over Germany.

Bomber Command was doing all it could to reduce the progress of the Third Reich against great odds wherever it could but sometimes it seemed there was just no luck left for us. Our own squadron took a heavy toll one morning through shear bad luck. The squadron was returning after a successful mission but the range had put them to the limit of their fuel. The really bad news was a Red Alert was in progress as they arrived back to land. As a matter of national security the complete black out could not be broken as German fighters were in the area, not even for a squadron of returning Hampdens. The pilots just didn't have a chance, they came in together but there was no runway to be seen. The radio operators must have been desperate. The planes ended up all over the camp. By daylight, the ridiculous mess was appallingly obvious. One had landed between two hangers, one ended up on top of a hanger and one just straddled the Bomb Dump entrance, other aircraft were littered about, just as if we had been hit by enemy bombers. It took days to clear up the wreckage.

Towards the end of August everyone knew our situation was desperate. How could we sustain the losses that were being inflicted and where were the aircraft that were needed? These were the questions with no answers but there was a limit and it was common knowledge that it was fast being approached. Everyone in the RAF at that time was at their wits end with the situation rapidly becoming a 'no hoper,' except, with one twist of fate.

On 25 August we put Berlin on the receiving end for the first time with ninety-five bombers on the first raid. A succession of raids were mounted over the next few weeks and not only on Berlin but on other German cities as well, but allied losses remained heavy. No one though could have perceived the overall effect of that raid and the successive ones but the true effect was realised in a couple of weeks. Us menial airmen were not to know or be told at the time but from information gained from innumerable and obscure sources it appeared Hitler had been incensed by the audacity of the underdog Britain bombing his beloved Berlin. On 6 September there were no raids, nor were there any raids for some days afterwards. The 'word' was he was so annoyed he ordered a complete change in Luftwaffe bombing strategy. He had ordered all attacks on British airfields should cease immediately and that massed bombing raids on London and major cities should commence as soon as possible. A few days later the raids started again but this time it was bombers and the targets were the major cities, especially London. This was a dire decision for the people of Britain, especially Londoners. It was certainly dire but the one redeeming factor was the Fighter Command had the pressure taken off them which gave the opportunity for them to recover and consolidate our forces. That's exactly what they did in an amazing turn around that enabled ever ready squadron units to attack large groups of relatively slow enemy bombers. The people of Britain were now to pay the price for this advantage but it was working. So much so we managed to inflict heavy losses to a German bombing raid on 15 September. The turning point had been turned but we continued having heavy losses by aircraft either getting shot down or 'go missing.' Some were lucky though, by either sheer courage or determination. Returning from a mission, Flight Lieutenant Goode, an Australian pilot had his nose shot off and one arm badly injured but his navigator brought the Hampden back and landed it safely. Later on he got decorated for it. Another navigator brought a Hampden back after the pilot got a cannon shell across his head, and they both lived to tell the tale. Out of all of them though, the most luckless one of these really grieved me and it also happened at Waddington. In mid October Burt took off on a mission with the Hampdens. I was in the Naafi at the time where you could only just hear the squadrons taking off, but on this occasion everybody on camp heard Burt's aircraft. About twenty seconds after take off fire broke out on board, a few seconds later a large explosion occurred at about 400 ft. The aircraft fell from the sky being disintegrated by a series of explosions from the fuel tanks and cylinders. One of the line mechanics saw it. When Burt's body was recovered it was found his parachute had been burned off him and virtually every bone in his body was broken. I think it's always the same with death; it always seems a greater tragedy when you knew them.

It was a tragedy to me. It wasn't so much the death but the fact it was such a waste of a good man from whom I had learnt so much. I wasn't given much time to grieve though, for apart from being kept busy with intensive bombing 'operations' the engine in my Hillman had just about laboured to its last. The big ends of the engine had started to knock and so I dismantled it to fit new bearings but I didn't have time to finish it before I received an unexpected posting in November to Boscombe Down. It was a bit of a surprise and I had to have a word with a flight mechanic I knew who said he would finish putting my engine together, then all I would have to do is pick it up. It was on such a low note that I left such a good station.

CHAPTER SIX
Research and Development

The war was beginning to affect the people at large in a manner not experienced before, as all the major cities continued to be bombed as the blitz on London increased. The whole system and way of life was changing. Now virtually everyone in any walk of life was affected one way or another by Britain being at war. The rationing and limitations so imposed by the Ministry of Food brought the message home at all levels, but as always, some more than others. The underlying facts were quite clear though, no matter who you were or what you were, everyone's way of life was under threat by a far worse alternative.

RAF Waddington had been a good station and considering the events at Nottingham, it had been a brilliant station really and it was with much regret that I was notified, for no reason that I was to be posted to RAF Boscombe Down. Even with its elevated 'Research and Development' status, if I was given a choice I would have stayed where I was. But as fate would have it on 20 November, a miserable day, I got off the train from Salisbury on to the station at Boscombe Down to look for the RAF transport to camp.

The place gave me a bad feeling even as I was arriving. I suppose the weather didn't help coupled with the fact I didn't have any aspirations about the place at all. It was a feeling that I was surprised about and disappointed with because it turned out to be well founded. It was a horrible place. As a new arrival I was allocated a billet in the satellite camp which unfortunately was still under construction and about ¾ mile away. It was literally being carved out of the hillside. The main camp had been established in peace time and looked OK. By the time I had reached my billet, I had mud splashed on my trousers from the knees downward and it hadn't been raining at all that day.

It took me a couple of weeks to realise just how miserable the place really was. On first arrival at my newly constructed wooden billet, with about twenty bed spaces, I wasn't too surprised to find it wasn't finished off. There was a lot of building and construction work in progress around the camp making virtually everywhere very muddy indeed. The only exclusions being Station Headquarters and the

Officers' quarters.

As a matter of course I was assigned to the Armoury where I met the armourment officer, Wing Commander Dark. He was one of those people who seem to fit their name; dark features, tall, one of the 'old school' types, quiet and therefore sort of dark natured. As it turned out, he was quite a decent chap really. In all there were about fifteen armourers but the flight I was allocated to consisted of Sergeant Woods, a Corporal and five airmen including myself. The Corporal, Watkins was alright and soon I was having a chat with one of the others who always answered to 'Jonas.' The Sergeant was a Londoner and although I hadn't met him before, I had a strong feeling he really liked the sound of his own voice. I didn't realise though just how much. Jonas was good enough to enlighten me a little.

'Oh, you needn't bother about him, he hasn't been in that long.'

'Good, but he's been made up quick.'

'Yeah, I know. I think it was something to do with him having worked in Fleet Street. I don't know though, but he's got a rare old opinion of himself. It makes me bloody mad at times. Here's me, with six years good service, as near as damn it. I have to teach him half the time. It just goes to show where a 'posh' accent and a load of waffle can get you.'

'Yeah, it sure does.'

I'd have got no points for guessing Jonas didn't like Woodsey very much but at times like this, a lot of units had some rare old mixes of personnel. We used to call Woodsey the 'Blimp' when he wasn't around due to his physical resemblance to the cartoon of Colonel Blimp. We got on alright with him but we were definitely not impressed and we used to drop him in it when we could. This was the general feeling amongst the other armourers as well, but opportunities when you could get away with it were rare.

Although several other units were based at Boscombe Down, the Armoury directly worked with the Bomber Development Unit. We were told its purpose was to improve bombing techniques generally but none of us knew what they were really playing with. Three bombers had been seconded for various trials, a Vickers Wellington (generally referred to as Wimpey's), an Avro Anson and an Armstrong Whitworth, Whitley. It was a new unit that was set up as an Aeroplane

RESEARCH AND DEVELOPMENT

and Armourment Experimental Development Unit and it was non-operational as regards bombing missions but there was plenty of flying to undertake the numerous tests and experiments they needed. The bombing range was at Lark Hill a few miles away.

After a few days, I knew this was not a good posting for me and therefore pursued a line of purposely avoiding making myself a 'good boy to have around.' This approach would then be in my favour to get another posting as soon as possible. What really got me down though was after a couple of weeks or more we still hadn't got any glass put in the windows. Even with the total war effort, I didn't think this would have been extravagant. I did think the laying of electricity cables in the ground might be a site more costly and therefore accepted the oil lamps we had to use were an enforced concession but after being there three weeks with the wind still blowing them out because there was still no glass in the windows, my opinion of the place reached rock bottom. With such basic accommodation I reckoned a moderate supply of hot water would definitely have been classed as a privilege and so tried to remove that desire, but it was hard to fulfil ones ablutions having to wash in cold water with an icy wind around ones middle! but even such a ridiculous place as this was to prove memorable for quite different reasons.

I was glad as it turned out that I had teamed up with Jonas who had been at the station for some time, long enough to get accommodated in the main camp. For as the bad weather turned to snow after a couple of weeks, the track to the satellite camp became a quagmire and Jonas was in the exceptional position as to be able to lend me a pair of gum boots. Those gum boots became my most treasured possession. They were invaluable.

What with such a miserable posting and such miserable weather, the thought of my old Hillman Minx seemed like that of a dear departed friend. I hadn't heard a word from the flight mechanic that I'd left it with and would have given a month's wages to have it back. I made a mental note to visit Waddington on my next leave.

As it turned out, there was always work for the ground crews out on the airfield but in the middle of winter it was no cushy number. The only recompense for this was that the Naafi van used to do a double tour to the various dispersals with coffee well fortified with rum. Often when I was working with another armourer called Alan we used to manage a timely arrival at several of the dispersals to coincide with the arrival of the Naafi van.

Early in December on a very muddy airfield at dispersal the Wellington was being loaded with a small bomb container via the bomb doors. For one reason or another we were a man short and it seemed 'Woodsey' was to join us for a change. The unit was about six feet long by eighteen inches square. It carried sixty incendiary bombs weighing four pounds each and therefore weighed at least 260 lb. The normal practice was for a man stood at each corner to lift the container so far, then for a fifth person to 'crouch' underneath it to lift it the last bit on his back, assisted by the others. It was a heavy load and it was customary that whoever was selected for the task always complained. On this occasion Sgt. Woods took it on himself to show us 'wimps' what a 'real' armourer could do and directed four of us to take the corners then lift the bomb container. At the right height we hesitated then he took the 'crouch' but instead of assisting him at the crucial moment we just let him take the full weight! We all watched him, for a good few seconds as he slowly sank into the mud offering a string of obscenities and impossible threats. Of course, after those 'few' seconds and with lots of sincere apologies we 'recovered' our grip. All he could do was fume and then walk off to the mess with further swearing and drawing strongly on his pipe whilst leaving muddy tracks across the peritrack. We didn't see him for the rest of the day. On the following day when we told Eric who served on the van about Woodsey getting muddied he thought it was so funny we got double ration!

Around this time old Wing Commander Dark proved himself to be not a bad old sod overall as one day myself and a couple of the others were on quite a cushy number in a hangar for a change. We were defusing 11 ½ lb practice bombs. This was done by unscrewing the tail section from the body which held the liquid that produced the thick white smoke when it was detonated. The tail took a No. 28 Detonator Burst which should be unscrewed in the armoury. To finally release the actual detonator it should be extracted with pliers, but a correct tap on your heel released it much quicker, saving a walk to the armoury. On this occasion old Wing Commander Dark walked in just as I was tapping the detonator out. I knew he'd seen me and reckoned that another 'charge' was looming. Dark was quite decent about it and said in a very firm voice 'this practice must cease immediately', then left. Considering that I could easily have been on a charge, I thought he was alright.

The only other recompense for being in such a miserable camp, as I saw it, was that as it was an experimental site, the work load was flexible and varied. This in turn led to all sorts of 'jollies', when we got rides in the aircraft on some sort of pretext of doing various 'air' checks. There was a serious side to it but in the light of world events it was a 'perk' to look forward to. As the station had a 'Research and Development' status we didn't always know just what tests or assessments were to be included but that was all part of the experience. It was usually, until my enthusiasm was somewhat dampened by a rather exceptional experience in the Wellington bomber (Wimpy). The Wimpey's fuselage was a geodetic construction which means it had extensive cross bracing which enabled it to support itself in the event of severe damage. In other words it could take an awful lot of punishment and still fly. Another interesting detail, at least for me as it turned out, was the fact there is a small air gap between the front gun turret and the fuselage.

This Wellington was going on a practice bombing run, assessing some new mechanism or other, I was told, so after clearing it with the Sergeant in charge, I took the opportunity of checking out the front turret. It was some distance to the target site and flying at 20,000 ft on an unusually clear sunny afternoon the unique patchwork quilt of England's countryside looked a very pleasant place. I could feel why the pilots enjoyed flying so much with the independence and superiority of height. After a little while I knew we would be approaching the target site and expected some changing of course and height adjustment. We turned a few degrees starboard then lost some height which was nothing unusual. Then the nose dipped abruptly which seemed a bit drastic for 'sighting', if that is what the pilot was doing. There must be a right pleb driving this one, I thought. But the nose continued to go down which was well out of order in anybody's books and as the horizon shifted to the top of the turret above my head it became evident that this was a down and out dive.

Larger bombers such as Wimpies were never designed with the idea of aerobatics in mind and a straight dive exerted an excessive amount of stress on the wings and air frame. Initially I thought the pilot was just messing about which didn't bother me too much as 18,000 ft is a safe height for any recovery. As the downward trend continued the altimeter started to really buzz round. By now a certain element of doubt crossed my mind so I put on the face mask with the microphone in it. I enquired of the pilot if he had lost just most of his marbles or his entire senses. Receiving only the crackle of static in the earphones, I energetically checked the intercom control and then noticed that the safe 17,000 ft was now a questionable 14,000 ft. Air speed was now climbing towards 290 mph. Then I noticed something that I'd never known before, I was nearly weightless. I could lift my whole weight on one arm. I was amazed for a moment, only a moment though when, back to reality I was shit scared. A large aircraft needs a lot of room to pull out of a straight dive and we were fast running out of it. The patchwork quilt that had been only a few moments ago was now straight in front of me and getting clearer and larger by the second. The roads and two farms were quite clear and I could tell the trees and hedges around the fields.

    I tried the intercom again to no avail but told the pilot what I thought of him just in case he could hear me. There was no point in panicking but I was getting very sticky with apprehension and suddenly felt very cold. The possibility of entering the fuselage crossed my mind, but there lay a problem as well. The hatch of the turret was not lined up with the fuselage so it wouldn't open, probably due to a damn valve 'letting by'. This trip was looking like a rather fatal decision. The altimeter was now at 8,000 ft with airspeed climbing to 330 mph and the whole thing was shaking terribly. I felt sick and briefly wondered just where Walter Briggs and Burt Hare were as I thought I would be joining them. That smart arsed flight mechanic would probably end up with my Hillman as well. And what about Elsie? Who would be telling her? And mum and dad? The countryside that had been before me had grown into just a few fields now, with one farmhouse to the right. By Hell, this'll wake 'em up! As the altimeter raced down to the 3,000 ft mark I had given up all hope and knew the end would be instant. Suddenly from nowhere I felt a desperate life giving twitch through my spine followed by a tremendous invisible weight that forced me into the seat. A second later with the 2,000 mark approaching I lost site of the farmhouse as the nose shifted a bit more and the 'G' force started to bite. And then it really bit, did it ever. It was so much that I couldn't move in my seat. God only knows how the plane had held together so far and to now pull so much 'G' was really pushing the luck, but I didn't mind. It was now groaning and creaking due to the strain but the engine tones deepened as they pulled us through to level flight with the trees not too far below. I started for the intercom once more to find out if I really did have a driver but the relief was so pleasant, I didn't bother.

After landing, we taxied to the hard standing where the engines were 'cut' and the crew got out. As the others headed for the 'ops room' the pilot checked behind to see that I had vacated the aircraft.

'You alright, Airman?' he addressed me.

'Yes Sir. Fine thanks.' Bastard!

'So young Butterworth got the pants frightened off him eh?' This was Sergeant Woods the following morning.

'Tell you what Woodsey. I bet you'd have had to take yours to the laundry in my place.'

'Rather you than me any day', chipped in young Jonas.

'Get away with yah.' Then, in his serious voice 'Right, I'm just off to Station Headquarters. See you after lunch.'

'Yeah, buzz off Blimp', quipped Jonas when Woodsey was safely out of earshot, then added 'If I had a bob for every time he had been up I wouldn't be able to buy a packet of cigs.'

'Tell you what Jonas my ol' fruit.' I said with a wry smile, 'Is his pipe and tin still on the bench?'

'Yes I think so.'

'Come with me.'

On a bench and using a stack of detonators for cover from the others, I told Jonas to finely chop a few rubber bands that I had.

'Right, let's have them. Pass me his tin.' I carefully introduced a different aromatic to Woodsey's favourite Shag tobacco.

'If you want to see the smile wiped off his face, get back early after lunch, it's guaranteed.' Jonas just smiled.

We returned early after lunch and were quite relieved to find a couple of the others there as well. A few minutes later Woodsey arrived prattling on about the mess food and the meals he used to have in Fleet Street. He casually picked up his pipe and tin from the bench and went into the armourer's crew room. We waited for about two or three very anxious minutes as he would be filling his pipe from his tobacco tin, then gently packing it down then closing his tin and reaching for his lighter. Right on cue, a sudden noisy bout of coughing started followed by some really prime swearing emanating from the crew room to the accompaniment of furniture being violently moved. Jonas and I both smiled in triumph. Woodsey emerged supporting himself in the doorway amid a bluish haze whilst holding his stomach. A remarkable pallor had replaced his usual smirk as with great effort in-between minor retchings he looked 'daggers' at the four of us present, searching for the slightest trace of amusement.

'If I ever find out who did this, I'll have his bloody guts for bloody garters!'

We all had the feeling that he really wanted to say more to us but he seemed to have a more pressing call for the toilets. His face really was a picture though.

In March I took some leave and called in at RAF Waddington to try and find either my car or the flight mechanic that I left it with. It was a rather optimistic mission as for months now the London blitz had continued with heavy bombing attacks on other cities and all the RAF stations were busy. I found my car all right but there was no trace of the mechanic. In the end, I totally wasted a full miserable wet day taking the damaged conrod out of the engine in a final effort to fix it but I needed more time and from the looks of things two tyres as well and better tools than I had with me. The car had to stay there and I continued on leave without it. When I got home, I had a word with my brother Llewellyn who said he would try and help me out with it. A couple of weeks later he drove down to Waddington with a friend and towed my poor Hillman all the way back to Upper Mill for me where I had a new engine fitted at Hughes and Bolton. The car was OK. My run of bad luck seemed to have taken a turn for the better as well around this time. In April I was very pleased and grateful to receive a posting to 90 Sqdn at West Raynham in Norfolk to which I had the most pleasurable experience of being able to drive to.

CHAPTER SEVEN

90 Squadron

In the middle of May at Easter time I finally arrived in Fakenham about 11.30 am a while before lunch and tested out what might be a good idea. I found the railway station and waited only a few minutes before I found a service truck going to the camp which I then followed right to the main gates. A smart idea for once. I booked in at the Guardroom and then started my arrival procedure at West Raynham. It seemed a very relaxed station with far fewer personnel than I would have thought but that may have had something to do with the fact that it was Saturday so I parked my car and started my arrival procedure. At that time, the word was that we were going to get some new aircraft but no one on the ground, so to speak, knew what aircraft were supposed to be having, we just knew that we were going to get some. It appeared that the RAF had at least manned the station in preparedness for 'them', but little else and therefore there was something of a general blasé attitude amongst the personnel. This fact was reflected by my final arrival stage at the Armoury which occurred at lunchtime. As I approached the door of the armoury it was abruptly pulled wide open as four or five blokes pulling jackets on noisily almost mowed me down in their eagerness to exit the premises. Realising the imminent possibility of a casualty, they loosely stopped.

'Sorry mate. You OK?' a ginger headed Corporal enquired.

'Yes. I think so.'

'Good. Who are you wanting to see?'

'Officer I/C I suppose. I've just arrived.'

'Ah, so you're joining us, well there are worse places. You want Willie, well Squadron Leader Watson that is.' The others were quickly growing impatient.

'Come on Ginge, you know they'll all be at lunch now, fill him in down The Swan.'

This seemed an encouragingly social suggestion and on his words it was evidently Nobbie that pulled up on his Norton motorbike. Ginge got on the pillion seat half sitting on the carrier leaving a gap between himself and Nobbie.

'Well, get on then. The Swan it is.' With that the three of us set off on the Norton to catch up the others already on their way. It wasn't quite how I remembered the 250cc Matchless handled, but it worked alright and we got there.

As we approached The Swan, we caught the others up who had gone on another motorbike and it was only then I realised that they had being towing the Sergeant on his bicycle as well. After getting a round of only half pints of bitter which I thought a bit unusual, Ginge introduced me to the others. No sooner had this been done when Nobbie suggested another round. With mutual agreement they all made their way out of the pub. I was amazed but followed them all very closely. As we got on the motorbike Ginge realised my puzzlement.

'What's the matter Kenny? We're going for another round. It's the beer shortage, he'll only serve us half a pint.'

'Ah, I see now.'

'Yes, we'll be nearly in Fakenham before we've had a couple of pints. Get on.'

'Right.'

During that first week I realised I'd joined a really good armoury crew. The Armourment Officer was W.Q. Tramere, Armourers Ernie Jones and Dick from Nottingham way and other lads on the different shifts. Just afterwards I found that Charlie Allen worked in one of the hangars. He was an Engine Fitter II E and we ended up being good friends and often used to go drinking together at a few pubs in Oundle village. Nobbie though was a bit of a character. He'd been in the service two or three years so was an old hand and knew 'what was what.' He always arrived on his old Norton ES2, you could hear him a quarter of a mile away, which usually meant that either he was late coming or he had left early. When he realized I'd had a bike a fair bit he was quite matey and many a time we swapped stories over a pint or so. When he knew the story of my mate Walter Briggs and another time how my gleaming 250cc Matchless had met its demise, and nearly mine, on the tram lines in Patricroft we were really good mates.

It was only a few days later on a warm and lazy, pleasant afternoon that apart from the general twittering of the Sky Larks on high and the occasional pigeon calling, the general quiet of the countryside was at work. In the fields the wheat and oats were straining upward and the potatoes were growing bigger while birds sang over the grazing cattle. From absolutely nothing, a rhythmic drone developed in the sky, deep and low on the horizon. It soon became evident to be coming from the west as it steadily grew into a vibrant monotone of engine noise. The approaching aircraft had not been seen in England before, flying low and descending on the approach to RAF West Raynham. With four engines and wings over-spanning the runway the wheels squealed on taking the load as Wing Commander J. Macdougall DFC landed the largest aircraft to arrive in Britain after crossing the Atlantic in a record time of 8 hours 26 minutes. It was the 14 May, Easter Monday and the first Flying Fortress B17 touched down to inaugurate Bomber Commands 90 Squadron in East Anglia. About four days later on 18 May two more Fortress's, AN 534 and AN 529 arrived followed a few days later by three more, AN 521, AN 523 and AN 527. The purpose was familiarisation and general training for the ground crews and a formal conversion for the air crews. On 12 May, the newly reformed 90 Sqdn had received the news from No. 2 Group, for reasons unknown to us, that it was to move from RAF Watton to West Raynham. This was to be an interim measure for finalising the preparations for their intended destination at RAF Polebrook in Nottinghamshire.

So it was about the 22 May I was travelling again. This time a group of us including Charlie, Dick from Nottingham and Ernie Jones were leaving West Raynham and going to RAF Polebrook which when I found out where it was, I thought it wasn't too bad as it was a sight nearer home! I did have my doubts though when I was told it was a new station, thinking back to Boscombe Down and the shortage of windows! We were to travel with a convoy of trucks with equipment along the A47 to the A1 then turn north and at Sawtry turn left off the A1 and along winding country roads to Polebrook. I'd probably have to take a 48 hours pass to get my car over later on, but that was no big deal. The camp seemed to be in the middle of nowhere but that was fairly usual. It was a new camp with one hanger but it looked as if another was being built and it was going to have three runways and service buildings north of the hanger. We never knew why we had moved station but it seemed OK with lovely countryside around, and a nice little village called Polebrook not far away and a really nice river

2. Boeing B17C also known as Flying Fortress 1
Copyright AirTeamImages.com

just beyond. In the few days before the Fort's arrived it was nearly like being on holiday! We were only really sorting equipment out and checking ammo stocks and types. As a group we sort of stuck together especially when checking out the local hostelries. This wasn't really difficult as we were all in hut 26. A twenty man standard wooden barrack hut. My bed space was number eighteen next to Ernie Jones number 19 with Charlie across the room and Dick further up. We soon checked out the village of Polebrook and a small town called Oundle not far away. All together it was a beautiful part of the countryside and with the warm summer weather, was idyllic. One day a few mates and myself, including Dick finished a bit early and went down to the river near Oundle to cool off and have a swim. We didn't think that the river would be deep at the edge because we didn't think how deep it was at all! Dick, full of enthusiasm was the first to strip off and jumped in, feet first just off the edge and went straight down. As he was the first we were still getting changed and didn't really notice that he hadn't come back up. After a little while, much longer than it should have been, I realised he was still down there! I dashed to the bank to look for him and could see his arms moving about but not coming up. I leaned right out and in the process of getting a dunking myself, just managed to grab his hand, and pulled him up. He was gasping like anything and looked terrible but there again, he had just all but drowned. He didn't go in after that, but he was a lot better after a cigarette. None of us needed any persuading to call at the Kings Arms on the way back to sample the tonic that Dick was so insistent he needed.

On 25 May Group Captain A.C. Evans arrived to open RAF Polebrook as self accounting, so we became the first airfield in England to operate Flying Fortress's B-17 C's or Fortress 1's as they were called. The first two or three weeks were fairly quiet really, as the aircraft hadn't arrived yet and there were only a few preparations one way or another so no real pressure. So, when myself and a new mate Ted were detailed to the Bomb Dump across the other side of the airfield, there didn't seem to be much reason not to cut across the runway. There were only acres upon acres of grass everywhere and the runway we had to cross to get to the bomb dump. There was a shorter runway that crossed the main one further up but in any event there was no flying today. To talk about luck on luck or not, what happened next was amazing or more to reality, pant changing stuff. We were having a chat and enjoying the countryside and were literally half way across the runway when we heard engine noise, which was unusual as we didn't have any aircraft. We weren't nearly on or nearly off the runway, but right in the middle. Within the few seconds we took to recognise it and turn around we were virtually face to face with the biggest beast of a bomber you could imagine just feet above the runway. This thing wasn't flying over. It was coming down, right on our runway, right for us and was as noisy as hell. The only thing to do was hit the deck, which we needed no prompting to do as it was over us and virtually on touch down. Even laid down we only stopped ourselves being blown along by spreading our arms and legs. Our berets were blown about 300 yds back. The first Fortress 1 had arrived from West Raynham. Two days later on 28 June, two more were flown to Polebrook, in advance of the main squadrons move there. It was a very impressive aircraft, very large, brand new and with four engines.

At the end of May morale generally picked up a bit as it became known that Germany's battleship the *Bismarck* had been sunk west of France and what with that and the arrival of the new bombers, the people in the area were talking about us winning the war in no time!

Progressively the other Fortress's arrived over the next couple of weeks and made the station look a bit more like an operational unit. About twenty arrived overall. As the numbers increased so did our work load with supplying ammunition, checking guns, checking different systems and changing ammunition type.

Each day the Fortress's were bestowed with servicing personnel, checking various equipment and instruments with engine tests and air tests being carried out. They had a General Inspection at 30 hours flying time then a Major Inspection after 100 hours and a Full Inspection after 240 hours. During the day, there was barely an hour went by when a couple of them weren't in the air with reports being done and aircraft fitters all over the place. The Americans were training our lads for the servicing ground-crews as well. May being the sort of month it is, with very changeable conditions especially higher up, day to day it tended to be either very good or very bad for flying especially at high altitude but fly is what they had to do. It was essential to get the training/conversion programme for the aircrews completed as soon as possible so the squadron could became operational. As an operational squadron the 'Forts' true advantage could be realised and that was to be able to bomb Hitler in Berlin, from a great height and with impunity which was a notion that delighted Churchillian ideals, another of which was that the Americans should become our allies at war. The machines had to work.

    It appeared to be an impressive squadron even though after seven days we still only had six aircraft, but what aircraft they were. Bristling with engines there was nothing else like them and their mere presence was a great boost for the morale of the station and the RAF as a whole. When I looked at them at dispersal I could only imagine that with a few squadrons of Fortress's, industrial Germany would quickly be bombed to a standstill. This view was endorsed by some very confidential information. The Fortress's were going to be equipped with the American's new Sperri General Bomb Sight which by their unofficial claim that 'it could hit a Herring barrel from 10,000 ft' had a reputation which preceded it. As all the aircraft were brand new, there were various trials and tests to be undertaken after which the American's would be part of the training/conversion programme for our Bomber crews, but fate was to deliver a blow which tarnished the image of these bristling bombers and undermined moral throughout the RAF. It wasn't obvious at first but barely four weeks after we arrived at Polebrook a devastating incident occurred that created the first doubts about the Fortress's design, that nobody cared to entertain. On 22 June, Fortress 1, AN522 Flown by Flying Officer J.C. Hawley took off from RAF Great Massingham near West Raynham, with a couple of Medical Officers on board to conduct altitude and flight tests. Somewhere high up over Yorkshire, about ten miles north of Catterick, the aircraft encountered problems and crashed. Little would have been known about the crash without the exceptional luck of Medical Officer Flight Lieutenant Steward who reported that the bomber entered a cumulonimbus cloud at 33,000 ft and became heavily iced up and hailstones the size of golf balls entered through the open gun ports after which it went out of control. On decent the port wing became detached and at 25,000 ft the fuselage broke in two. It was only the fact that Flt. Lt. Steward was travelling in the rear fuselage that enabled him to successfully bail out at 12,000 ft. It took a while for the details to filter through to us but it was a concern. Things didn't get much better either as on 3 July Fortress 1, AN528 was destroyed when a troublesome engine caught fire, after its 100 hours inspection during a late night ground run. During this time another Fortress 1 crashed during an altitude test and yet another caught fire. As armourers we had about five weeks of training and gunnery practice duties before the first real bombing mission. Everyone had started off fired up with enthusiasm for the Fort's but after the second high altitude incident serious reservations were being murmured about them and none of the ground crew would ever go on altitude tests, some just being reluctant to even fly in them!

Whatever reasons the powers that be had to bless the Royal Air Force with the Flying Fortress bomber, they certainly caused a lot of disturbance, excitement and unfortunately, disappointment. To many people though, the arrival of a few of these technological wonders was a mere novelty as the actual numbers involved were low even by a squadron's standards and we were not trained up or kitted out for them and above all the Americans were still not yet committed to the war. To the film companies though, that minor detail wasn't going to stand in the way of them making a 'fast buck' as we found out by a surprise order one day.

'Butterworth.'

'Yes, Sergeant?'

'You and Harris there, go with Corporal Jackson. There's a couple of film men with cameras, they want a few shots of 500 lb.ers on bomb trolleys.'

'Hey, come on Kenny looks like we could be famous!'

I didn't want to disappoint him but I just knew that nobody was going to make a couple of RAF erks famous. Still, we did as we were directed and spent the best part of 3 hours either standing around a couple of bomb trolleys with 500 lb.ers on them or sitting on them in thirty different ways, all in front of a Fortress. We didn't see hide nor hair of any film stars even though Richard Greene was supposed to star in it but we were definitely filmed on the bombs being loaded.

Daylight bombing operations commenced on 8 July, when three Fortress's set off for Wilhelmshaven on the German coast, a long way from Berlin. Conditions were good but only two aircraft reached the target area and only one attacked. Enemy fighters were spotted but the Fortress' waist guns had frozen to their mountings. Survival was only achieved because the fighters turned away. A layer of ice 7 in. thick on the tail plane of the third aircraft had forced an early return to base. It was not the successful mission that had been hoped for.

The Flying Fortress's defence was four 0.50 in. (12.7 mm) machine guns, two waist, one tail, and a single 'bathtub' machine gun housing on the lower fuselage. There was one 0.30 in. (7.62 mm) machine gun in the nose. While all the activity was going on around the Fortress's, I was on routine duties in the Armoury with a few others. One of the better duties we had was odd trips in twin engined Blenheims towing drogue targets for Forts target practice, towed with something like piano wire. Drogue targets were hand winched in and out of the aircraft and towed about 300 ft behind if you were lucky as some of us had one or two near misses, once someone actually hit the wire and the target was lost! Of course there was lots of talk about the capabilities of the 'Forts' and what they could or would not do and a snippet of information that I picked up gave me the first niggling doubt as to the real value of these gleaming and impressive aircraft. Apparently the RAF wanted the maximum possible flying height so they would be immune from the defending German 109E and 109F fighters. But to do this they had to compromise on bomb load to get the height. Officially the bomb load was 4,800 lb but that was for the Americans ceiling height of 20,000 ft. The maximum bomb load at 30,000 ft was much less, about 2,000 lb not even a Ton of bombs. Compared to a Whitley Bomber it was not a lot.

It was no wonder the Yanks were using a super accurate bomb sight, with so few bombs, they'd have to make everyone count, But the problems were not to end there, if Berlin was to be bombed from a great height, to operate from over 30,000 ft, needed a well heated aircraft, ample oxygen and clear weather for bombing accuracy. Huge oval shaped gun ports in the aircraft's sides, when opened, flooded the fuselage with air as cold as -50°C. and a non pressurised fuselage meant an elaborate oxygen system, portable bottles and heavy clothing. Hand traversed guns were certainly going to be a challenge at high altitudes and any hazy weather at all, would be a problem. What was never in short supply was the courage and will to attempt to make the Fortress a going concern. For even the most patriotic of us though, sometimes we had to revert to blind faith. The possibility of reaching Berlin in daylight to deliver a puny load could never boost morale and because of the risks, Fortress's could only operate mainly against fringe targets. Had the weather been better, Berliners might have witnessed the white vapour trails of the Forts which would surely have attracted wrath and vengeance.

In July I finally got my promotion to Leading Aircraftman and still had my Hillman and being a fairly sociable lad with a sound appreciation of good beer, it wasn't long before I became acquainted with some of the locals. Of course, as I had a car, suggestions for trips out were always plentiful and I enjoyed many a good night out over a game of darts or my favourite, bar skittles where you use a wooden ball suspended on a string. One night in particular I went to the pub in Oundle with Ian to pick up Dick who was coming back from leave. The difference today though, was we were on some bicycles for a change. It might have been that I'd forgotten that I said I would pick him up but either way we were in Oundle with bicycles. While we were waiting we met some mates and after a few beers were joined by Dick. He was well pleased to see us but somewhat disappointed when I told him about the bicycles. A pint or two seemed to pacify him a little and eventually we started back with him pedalling and me on the cross bar. I think he would have preferred to be steering at this time of night. Probably something to do with the amount of beer we'd had but I'm not sure it would have made much difference as it was close to pitch black outside. Cycling with a few wobbles back from the pub and with no lights and a 'blackout' in force we were lucky to stay on the road. We started getting along quite nicely but unfortunately we weren't the only ones out on the road in the pitch black as we found out when we were hurled off the bike and into the hedge. If we weren't actually hurled into the hedge it certainly felt like it but the source of our catastrophe was blatantly clear even in the pitch black. Whatever we had run in to instantly cried out in pain and fell to the ground with a large thud along with ourselves and then started swearing and cursing like billy-o and threatening to charge us with a string of offences including attempted murder (again!). It only transpired that we had just happened to run into and knock over the village 'Bobby.' He was quite mad at first but when he realized we were in the RAF and hadn't been paid so I couldn't tax my car to pick up my best friend who had just come back from a family bereavement, he was quite reasonable about it. He sympathized a little bit but maintained that he'd have to 'book' us now because of the damage to his uniform.

'I'm sorry sunshine,' he said 'but I'm going to book you for this, now. You've had a good run for your money with that car of yours.' I later got fined 5s.

There was always common topics that warranted discussion and none so much as the position of our armed forces and Germany to the government and what they should be doing, and from the weather to the price of bread, beer, and petrol, which had been on ration for about eighteen months now. There were always a few folk that wanted to make things a little easier or get an advantage of some sort, especially when it came to fuel. The aircraft fuel was coloured purple to deter people from using it as it was so easily identified, and also illegal. So it was that after careful negotiations with selected clientele (farmers), sometimes we used to exchange their stationary engine fuel, for our Pool petrol. A friend of mine, an armourer who used to live in Oundle and knew the area was the chief negotiator. During the day aircraft petrol was left in five gallon drums out at dispersal by a friendly and entrepreneurial Flight Mechanic then at night I would drive out to dispersal and get the drum in my boot, then drive to the farm and exchange it. We didn't do many of these 'operations' but they were most desirable when any of us was doing a trip home. About the middle of July I managed to fix a couple of days leave with a 48 hours pass as well and set off for the Commercial Hotel to get a little more acquainted with Elsie whose sister, Mary, Llewellyn was courting. I'd worked out that because it was my squadron that had received the latest type of bomber, I'd have plenty of excuses for not writing as much as I should have. So I'd probably have an easy time of it.

CHAPTER EIGHT

With the Army

Since Norway had fallen to the Germans, they were using Oslo as a staging post to attack the North Atlantic convoys and news had come through that the Admiral Von Scheer had been located at the docks in Oslo. All that us ground crews were told was that we had 24 hours notice of a detachment to RAF Kinloss on the east coast of Scotland which had been the No. 19 Operations Training Unit and in an amazingly short space of time the detachment of Fortress 1s, was on its way. We were close behind in setting off but it was going to take us about 11 hours longer than the squadron as we were allocated travel warrants for the train. From setting off at 6.15 am we didn't sign in at RAF Kinloss until 7.45 pm. None of us could ever remember being so bored for so long. The camp had only been built a couple of years earlier; it had three hangers and a mixture of technical buildings and the armoury. It was supposed to have been a Flying Training School away from the operations over East Anglia but then nobody thought we'd have a national threat from the direction of Norway. It was a good station with excellent food and at the time the weather was beautiful and hot. This was the primary training unit for bomber crews and at any one time there were people from all over the place. It's situated well up the coast and only just inland from the sea. One of the first 'rumours' we found out was the airfield sometimes got flooded by the sea from Findhorn Bay. The accommodation wasn't very good but they did have glass in the windows! It turned out there wasn't much of a variety in the menu but that was compensated a little by the fact that there were at least a few hotels in the town. We hadn't been there two days before the first attack was launched against the German '*Admiral Von Scheer.*'

On 5 September four Fortress's set off to attack the *Admiral Von Scheer* in Oslo harbour with a high altitude bombing run. It was a day or two later that we got the details of the raid. Apparently one came back early with supercharger trouble, the other, unable to spot the ship bombed the docks from 30,000 ft. The remaining two had limited success.

On the 8 September a second raid on Oslo was launched that

nearly ended operations because they were intercepted by enemy fighters. One was shot down, another disappeared and the only one to reach the target found it obscured by cloud and thus brought its bombs back. The fourth suffered enormous punishment, one gunner being killed and the other wounded. One engine was put out of action, the other three were all damaged and the aileron controls were shot away. Against all expectations, Sgt. Woods (aircrew) reached Kinloss, but the experience confirmed the RAF's worst fears about high altitude bombing and it was going to be the Americans that would have to perfect the techniques. Captain Mathieson was the senior pilot on the Forts with the USAF and was attached to 90 Sqdn. He gave a talk over the radio about the bombing of the ship from 37,000 ft soon afterwards. There wasn't a lot of activity for the Forts after the second raid and we just started operations with Blenheims doing a lot of practice bombing which still involved the preparation, bombing up, practice and observations. When the aircrew were doing the 'circuits and bumps' in training I often had a few jolly's stood in-between both pilots in the astra dome. As there were about twelve or so armourers we weren't over worked and found a bit of time in the evenings to socialize in the localities of Forres, Nairn and Elgin. I know it was a good job that it was a short detachment as I knew a lot more about whiskey by the time we left!

By the same token that 90 Sqdn was here on detachment, so there were personnel from all sorts of other trades like cooks, bandsmen, MT drivers and aircraft fitters and the like. As we were the first squadron to operate Fortress's so a lot of other folk were far from familiar with them. In the normal course of events this wouldn't matter too much as instruction would always be given. There was one serious exception to this that related to giving them enough room. There were a few four engined bombers in service but also there were two engined bombers and it was the outside engines that needed to be well noted especially when manoeuvring on the hard standing or loading. You might think you couldn't fail to notice them but when there was so much noise going on from so many aircraft it wasn't that easy. On one occasion one of the bandsmen that were on general duties was waiting for a team mate and was idly watching the preparation of a Fortress. In this instance another aircraft was manoeuvring close by and some

Corporal had shouted instructions to him, which he couldn't hear but the Corporal was indicating something behind. The Bandsman turned round to see what he should be doing then stopped dead. I was in the front nose of another aircraft adjusting some mountings and I could see what was about to happen as I suddenly felt sick. The chap's body momentarily froze as like a butchers slicing machine on meat and amid a spray of blood the tremendous propeller sliced the front half of his head off. His body dropped to the deck. There was a bit of a panic after that as a few people had seen what had happened but couldn't communicate due to the noise. A few minutes later though an Ambulance arrived and the engines were turned off on the aircraft being made ready. The Fortress involved was directed to a parking area close by. We found out later that when the pilot had got out of the aircraft and he was informed by ground crew staff of the incident he broke down in dismay. He had been completely unaware of the accident. The incident was recorded as an accident.

No one could say what decisions had been taken by the RAF while we were at Kinloss but we had gone on detachment with Fortress 1's with a view of going after the *Admiral Von Scheer* in Oslo but were now returning with Blenheim IV's. It was like they had been 'dropped' like a hot potato. A detachment of Fortress 1's was posted to the Middle East in October 1941. I don't know that many people were disappointed though, but Blenheim's were pretty steady aircraft. I managed to cadge a ride back to Polebrook in a Blenheim when the Squadron detachment was returning to Polebrook but the only available space was in the bomb bay. By train it would have been a nine to ten hour journey, but in a Blenheim it was a two hour trip so it was well worth a little discomfort.

As our regular crew returned to Polebrook there seemed to be a bit of an anti-climax as there was nothing really new or exciting and the bombing runs were more routine, I got a forty-eight hour pass to see my family and Elsie and Mary and see how things were at home.

Since we all had returned from Kinloss there appeared a subtle change to our daily routine had occurred, courtesy of the CO which took the form of a general daily inspection or parade of the ninety to one hundred personnel there. Needless to say it wasn't very popular and serious questions were raised as to why it was only instigated now, since the Americans had left. But, occur it did and it didn't really cause too much of a problem as it always took place at 0800 hrs. On one occasion however the parade was called early, for reasons we'll never know, and the CO was inspecting. It didn't go too bad until he ordered our coats to be opened. Only then did he conduct his inspection and when he saw how many various forms of apparel including pyjamas were worn in place of uniforms he decreed a general charge of 'improperly dressed' to selected present company. That certainly included myself, which started me off on what was to be a six week term of jankers. For this offence, we all had to do Pack Drill for one hour in the mornings for one week. Eleven people got charged and given one week jankers.

One evening, about late November Charlie, myself and another mate Ian went on one of our frequent visits to Oundle. It was a very nice small town, or a large village with a large open market place with an old hall or something in the middle and shops and pubs on the roads around it. Normally Ernie would have come with us but we all knew he was on Guardroom Duties as we had seen him on the way out. It was nothing special in Oundle, we'd have two or three pints and a chat, sometimes with the locals then head off back. Sometimes we'd call in at the Kings Arms in Polebrook village on the way back. On this occasion by chance we stopped for a quick one before closing time. There were a few people in the bar but it wasn't too busy so we got a pint and almost straight away recognized a familiar voice from around the corner of the bar whittling on to some unfortunate local about social history or something. I say 'whittling on' because if the truth be told he was as pissed as a fart but there was no mistaking the voice of young Ernie Jones. That in itself was somewhat surprising but a far greater concern was that he was supposed to be on Guardroom Duty and was not allowed off camp in the first place. Young Ernie was only just eighteen years old but he was married with a three month old baby. He always seemed a bit naive but there was nothing naive about him tonight, he must have been packing them away like there was no tomorrow.

'Bloody hell, Charlie. What shall we do? If we leave him here he'll get charged AWOL.'

'I don't know.'

Ian chipped in with a profound idea considering it was 10.30 pm. 'If we get him on to camp, he can't be AWOL can he?'

'I suppose not.' We all agreed.

'So we need to get him on to camp when we sign in at the Guardroom' he continued.

We all agreed that's what we should do.

'Right.' Charlie started. 'Kenny, when you get to the gate stop your car just down a bit. When we get out to sign in, you and I will occupy the duty corporal while Ian gets Ernie out of the other side then joins us to sign in. And Ernie can get off to the mess.'

At that time of night it sounded like a magic idea! So off we set.

We managed to get Ernie out of the pub and into the car and headed for camp. Stage one worked. I stopped the car just down a bit so it was a bit less obvious from the Guardroom. Charlie and I got out and headed for the 'signing in' window and the Duty corporal. Ian got out as well but nipped round the other side to let Ernie out. Within seconds, Ian was with us to sign in as well. Stage two was complete! Things were looking good but it quickly became evident that our impromptu planning had underestimated Ernie's commitment to our friendship and loyalty. From nowhere, there he appeared just smiling at everyone and gently swaying. He stood next to Ian to 'book in.' Suddenly I wanted a very big hole to open up beneath me. The Corporal sort of double checked his recognition of the lad in the poor light.

'Oi. You're Jones!' This is it, I thought. Quickly I realised that this wasn't 'it' though. Ernie hadn't picked the pencil up because he was just stood there, swaying and fumbling with something, and smiling! We were a bit worried as well we might be, because all this was completely unpredictable. Without so much as a 'by your leave' or anything, he had released his old 'John Thomas' and proceeded to wash the duty desk and the signing in book with a copious amount of processed bitter! It was just obvious this was a 'first' for the Duty Corporal. He was transfixed, almost stunned with incomprehension of what he was seeing. He was, that is for about four or five seconds. Then that really was 'it.' None of the military police were small blokes and ours was no exception. He leaned forward through the window with both arms out-stretched, grabbed Ernie's shoulders and just hoisted him in through the window. He was really cursing and swearing at Ernie and amongst others things told him he was under arrest! This was a complete failure of stage three. By now the Corporal was a bit more rational though and shouted to us 'three,'

'In here!' We knew he was well annoyed so didn't hang about.

'Wait there!' he demanded.

'You. Airman!' He shouted, with a fair old grimace. 'Name and number.' Ernie had stopped smiling now but he was still swaying about a bit. He managed to get his name out OK but each time the Corporal checked his number it came out different.

'Right,' said the Corporal. 'You're not messing me about. In the cells with ya,' and with that he opened the cell door and Ernie stepped in. Things weren't looking good for Ernie, but considering we'd only been for a drink, things weren't looking too good for us either. As luck would have it, the telephone started ringing in the office next door.

'Charlie,' I said. 'He doesn't know his number. We could let him out and he won't know who he was.' While there wasn't time to think about it, this seemed a devilish idea.

'OK,' we nodded in agreement. Charlie let Ernie out and pushed him out of the Guardroom, then came back and waited with the rest of us. When the Corporal came back the double take he had to do was 'a picture.'

'Right, you bastards. What have you done with him?'

'We've just signed in, Corporal.'

'Someone's going to be in trouble now, and it ain't me.' He paused. 'You three, in there,' indicating the cell. He went to my car and had a look through it and came back with a military issue overcoat, with the last three numbers of the owners service number written in it 152. Mine were 694 (972694) and Charlie's and Ian's were different. He made a phone call and within two minutes four more very expectant RAF police arrived. The corporal checked his book and made some comment about it not being ours but then made some sort of exclamation about Hut 26. We were all accommodated in Hut 26. My bed was 18 and EJ's bed was 19.

'Right,' he said to them. 'Take these three to their billet, number 26 and arrest everybody inside. All names and numbers.' There was no way out of this one so we went straight to the billet. We went in, the lights went on and everyone was woken up and ordered out of bed. The entire billet complied except one. Snoring his head off, still fully clothed and with a cover just pulled over him Ernie was now oblivious to the current proceedings, just possibly due to the amount of beer he'd had. They woke him up eventually and continued to arrest him and the three of us as well! We were all taken back to the guardroom and locked up for the night.

In the morning all of us were brought before the CO individually, on various charges. It seemed a bit suspicious to be tried individually, especially Ian, Charlie and me. Ernie had loads of charges against him; breaking out of camp whilst on Fire Picket, breaking into camp, urinating on guardroom property, being drunk and disorderly and dereliction of duty plus a couple more! Ernie spun such a tale about being a regular church goer, only being eighteen and a little naive about the 'ways of the world' (but not too naive to have a three month old daughter!) and not drinking before and so on that the CO felt sorry for him and he only got three days loss of privileges. Mine on the other hand were conspiracy to disrupt, coercion of a junior rank, disobeying a direct order and incitement of anarchy. I was charged as being the ring leader because 'it was your car, and you were driving.' I didn't think it would 'cut any ice' to say I was just trying to help a mate out so I got a lecture about 'doing ones duty' and 'patriotism' then got twenty-eight days jankers. The others got seven days loss of privileges each. I was getting really 'cheesed off' with British justice and decided to apply for an overseas posting at the first opportunity. My 'jankers' period started on 23 November which wouldn't normally matter as a general period of misery but world events just two weeks later turned everyone's head. The entire camp and I'm sure the whole of Great Britain was shocked to reality by devastating news that filtered through and was in every newspaper. Initial reports claimed that Japan had bombed America without any declaration of war and as a result America had directly declared war on Japan. When further details were revealed it appears that on 7 December the entire Japanese air force had bombed the American Naval Fleet while it was moored in Hawaii in the Pacific Ocean. We had all known that Japan had been at war with China. But for America to be at war with Japan changed everything. It seemed like the world was at war. This idea wasn't too far from the truth as on 11 December Germany and Italy declared war on America. There was going to be a lot more trouble from now on.

My twenty-eight days jankers finished just before Christmas, thank goodness and just like I'd decided earlier, I applied for an overseas posting, anywhere! With the jankers finished though, at least I'd be allowed my leave to go home for Christmas but there was a sort of bonus before that.

To introduce a little 'festive spirit' to the camp the competitive sort, a football match had been arranged between two teams, one from the Aircrew and one from Station Headquarters, (SHQ). Everyone that was available was invited to attend including armourers! It wasn't a bad game in one sense and normally all the non-commissioned ranks would be 'rooting' for SHQ. I know that the SHQ lot did loads of fouls but because I'd just done nearly six weeks of jankers, mostly between the guardroom and SHQ, I deliberately became a 'turncoat' and cheered on the Aircrew team. I think it was the following day I set off for the 'Commercial Hotel' in the trusty Hillman. I'd been home for a weekend about ten weeks ago so I reckoned that while I didn't talk about 'work,' I'd be alright. I'd been lucky and avoided any guard duties over Christmas so I managed to get four days leave.

It was a funny sort of time to be going home though. Well it at least felt different and I suppose that made it different. A lot of things had happened and changed in just over a year, a lot of things. I was a different person going home from the person I was when I last left. The home was the same, the parents and brother were the same but the person returning, me, was different. It bothered me that I felt so different because I loved my family and our home. During the drive back I think I sort of resolved the case with the conclusion that I'd probably grown up a bit, and if that was the only difference then things were still pretty good. I really wanted this to be the case because Llewellyn had been married to Mary for nearly two years now and her sister Elsie and her mother seemed to be doing a bit more than looking in my direction. It was certain they'd all be there when I got back (or soon after) and I'd have to come up with a bit of 'flannel' as to why I'd hardly written. I was pretty relieved that I'd managed to keep all of the last month's situation from Elsie as I was bound to see her over Christmas. What with Elsie and Mary being sisters and their mother being friends with mum and dad, it was in my own interests to think carefully about what I said to anybody. As luck would have it though, the only topic other than rationing was about Japan bombing the American fleet at somewhere called Pearl Harbour in the Pacific Ocean. Time just flew by. We all had a nice Christmas and Elsie visited each day but in absolutely no time at all, I was due back to camp.

At camp it had become general knowledge that 90 Sqdn was going to be disbanded really soon and with the news of America 'joining' the war speculations were rife throughout the camp. By the 12 February virtually everyone had received their postings to somewhere or other. Mine was to RAF Kidlington. For the first day or so after I'd got my notification I felt a bit uneasy about it as RAF Kidlington was the home of the 102 Operational Training Unit (Glider Unit), part of the 3rd Airborne Division. For the first part I was thinking what is an Armourer going to do with a load of gliders! The second part of the thinking was the Airborne Division was the Army. It seemed that I was going to join a load of paratroopers. I didn't know how interesting it was going to be but it would certainly be different.

So it was in the middle of February that the little Hillman and myself found our way to Oxford in the afternoon. That was pretty good as Kidlington village and the camp were just a few miles further up on the Banbury Road. Just as I was leaving Kidlington I turned left into Langford Lane to arrive at 102 Operational Training Unit (Glider Unit) 3rd Airborne Division. I was lucky to get my arrival signatures completed by teatime. It was quite a large camp with a lot of hangers and only a steady walk from Kidlington, so that scored serious points. Initially I was billeted on camp but I knew the satellite accommodation site was barely a mile away so I decided to make that one of my primary objectives at the first possible opportunity. At the beginning of February news came through that the Japanese had invaded Singapore and only took a week to do so. It didn't look good.

The following day I found the Armoury and reported for duty. I wasn't sure just what the set up was but there were two 'Officers In

Charge,' Captain John Blatch and Captain Peter Stancliff. I think they alternated or something. There was a nice workshop there as well, which looked very appealing. Sergeant Blake and Sergeant Edwards were instructors who were in charge of a small armoury allocated to the training division. There was myself and several other armourers there to support them. Apart from normal routine duties of issuing, cleaning, checking and receiving weapons etc, there would be a variety of training projects to do. Apparently the purpose of the station was to train the Paratroop Regiments in airborne assault techniques using gliders. I'd always thought of gliders as being one and two man planes but the ones here were enormous. There were three different types used, the 40-seater Horsa's and Hamelcars and sometimes 9-seater Hotspurs. The Horsa's and Hamelcars were a bit similar and very large. The Horsa had an 88 ft wingspan and a 67 ft fuselage. It had a door on each side of the fuselage, on the Port side in front of wing and on the Starboard side behind the wing. The tail section was designed to be removed so that ramps could be used to load and unload. I thought it was a clever idea that a cordex explosive could be used to blow the tail off, like when they had to deploy quickly on an assault or something. The Hotspur had a 45 ft wingspan and could accommodate eight fully armed troops and a cargo of 1,660 lbs. One of the first things I was reprimanded on was for calling the glider pilots, pilots. For a reason no one really explained, it was a fact that the glider pilots were indeed called Coxswain's. I was certainly not going to change things but coxswain just didn't have the clean sharpness that 'pilot' did. The training projects ended up being quite interesting. I did a few special jobs. One was to make a scale model of the practice assault landscape and features of the training area. This was used for the purpose of briefings and debriefings. One of the really interesting jobs was to make sectioned demonstration pieces of guns and grenades, as required for training. It was hard work and took a long time but the finished piece was always individual and showed how equipment worked that just couldn't be seen otherwise. There were various other devices I covered that were a bit different. The Time Pencil for one. This was like a rather large fat pencil but was in fact an explosive metal stick. It was armed by squeezing or squashing it, when an acid was released internally which 'ate' through to the explosive. They were colour coded to determine the delay of the fuse for various uses e.g. for destroying aircraft, arsenals or buildings etc. One of the Anti-personnel devices was a small steel container with a spike or plunger on top. When the plunger was depressed, it operated a light creep spring which in turn pushed a firing pin into an upturned .38 cartridge, which shot out vertically. It wasn't a very nice concept, but we were at war. The duties weren't always so interesting. One of the regular jobs was to be on night duty to be available to issue or receive weapons and ammunition. It was a regular thing that the 'Coxswain's' would have night time flying exercises for two reasons. When they were on missions over enemy territory they would have to land without lights and when landing at RAF or Army bases they would land on prepared 'flare paths.' Then, the duty armourer might be on the airfield, as required. The Hawker Hector aircraft which were used as the tugs had an electrical flare on the wing and one of our duties was to check the flare on landing and disconnect it. One evening I was on duty on the airfield and sometimes there was a lot of activity but sometimes it was so boring that even a glider landing in the dark was something of interest. This particular evening was a very quiet one and the only activity was some servicing work taking place on aircraft across the runway, on the hard standing. The fact that an engine fitter was crossing the 'flare path' was incidental. It was incidental until I saw a Horsa silently appear through the night cloud in the distance. I could see the direction the fitter was walking in and he had his back to the oncoming Horsa. If I had shouted, he may have heard me but he wouldn't have understood anything as I was some distance away and if he could have seen me, which he couldn't, he wouldn't have known what I was indicating. The Horsa was coming in on the flare path which although they weren't terribly bright, the brightness of the flares on either side left the runway in-between looking quite black against which a dark uniform just wouldn't be seen. It would be surprising if the fitter would hear anything at all and as the Horsa was getting lower and closer, the fitter was progressing across the runway, but not quick enough. From a distance it may have been that the glider could just do a 'hop' at the last minute, or may be not. The Horsa had almost touched down just as it impacted with the fitter three quarters way across the runway. The leading edge of the wing was about five feet from the ground. I watched dumb struck as his head was bounced clean over the top of the wing as his body dropped lifeless. I set out to contact the guardroom but seconds later I heard shouting from the incident area. A few minutes later an ambulance arrived and duly put the body and then the head on a stretcher and drove off. It was a very sobering incident but in my ignorance, I couldn't help thinking as the ambulance drove off, 'the wonders of medical science!'

After a couple of weeks I did get a letter off to home and bring 'them' up to date with how things were and was careful to only ever mention aspects which were reassuring. Since Christmas, mum and dad, especially mum thought it would be a really good idea for me to invite Elsie to the cinema or to a dance or something when I next was home. She seemed a nice girl well enough and I have to admit we did get on OK over Christmas but I wasn't certain just how much that had to do with Llewellyn being married to her sister, Mary. I guess I'd see how things were next time.

It wasn't too long before I managed to get a billet on the satellite camp. This may have been expedited by the fact that our armoury corporal, Brian Sayle was I/C one of the satellite dormitories. It was no big deal really but by and large personnel there were left to there own devices and there was rarely any trouble. So generally speaking you could come and go as you please and, if there was any emergency on camp, it would be those currently living on camp that would be called first, so all in all it was a good move. The billets were fairly standard war time wooden built huts of a single large dormitory with twelve or eighteen beds in it with a Corporal in Charge who had a small individual room at the entrance. It was only after I'd moved to the satellite camp that I really started chatting with Brian, mainly because there was time in the evenings. I can't really say we had a lot of things in common but we did get on quite well. I wasn't impressed by the fact that he was from London but the fact that his father was directly connected to Fox Films was interesting. I think I scored a few points with him when I told him about the film *Flying Fortress* starring Richard Green and how some of it was shot at RAF Polebrook. I told him that if he was quick he'd see me on the opening shots next to the bomb trolleys but in truth I didn't know if I was on it or not! We got on OK and he was very good company after a 'couple of pints,' so we frequently went for a drink in Oxford.

The course for the army Parachute Regiment was six to seven weeks. In that time, the designated 'Coxswains' would learn to fly the gliders. The other personnel and the Coxswains would receive weapons training, map reading lessons 'in the field' and demolition techniques etc. The whole course culminated in a Passing Out Exercise in which a platoon would take off with Hawker Hector planes towing the gliders and fly to the exercise area about nine miles away. They'd be assessed on their landing and then they'd have to 'storm' a designated and well defended farm house or ruin necessitating the demolition team to use a 2 lb 'slab' of gelignite to blow it up. Afterwards they would have to reposition the Hawker Hector tugs and gliders, hitch up, take off and return. There was an alternative exercise where they would land near a river and have to make their way upstream on one side against an opposing group, cross by a rope bridge at a designated point and 'take control' of a barge cum pontoon, navigate back down the river to the pick up point and board the aircraft and return.

Quite often I used to accompany the course on map reading exercises because it was pretty good fun and a pretty good skive! I managed to wangle it so that I took part in the passing out exercises as well, the teams didn't mind as I had a bit of inside knowledge on the course, so to speak. By and large the first few months went by fairly well. The work was interesting, I'd got in to the satellite camp, Oxford had turned out to be a fairly sociable town and I had got on with Elsie pretty well on my last 48 hours pass. We had got on well enough for 'long term' commitment to be mentioned, which was alright in itself but I still felt a bit uneasy that I was getting prompted by Llewellyn and sometimes Elsie had a really workable 'plan' for anything that cropped up.

CHAPTER NINE

The Knife

Sometime around June, the Horsas were deployed to another station to be part of a Heavy (Glider) Conversion Unit and our station was redesignated as No. 5 Glider Training School on 30 June. This didn't really affect our work and things just carried on as they were with visits to Oxford and Kidlington and the odd 48 hours pass home. On the next pass home I had, my relationship with Elsie really did progress somewhat but I'm still not sure how much of it was to do with me! We had been out a few times and as her sister was married to Llewellyn and her mother was friends with my mum and dad there wasn't much 'new ground' to make but above all, there was a lot of people getting killed in this war, both at home with the bombing and abroad and no one felt easy about it. My mother, on one of her little chats, as you might expect did mention that if there was a wedding, how wonderful it would be for the whole family especially in these darker times. So when I mentioned the idea to Elsie she was over the moon with it and didn't mind at all that I didn't have an engagement ring on me, blaming it all on the war and 'austerity' measures. I was to be married. Over all I came back feeling quite good about things and the following day I felt quite enthusiastic about it when I told Brian in the pub. It was alright telling him but he didn't behave the way I had expected. He didn't come out with anything like 'congratulations' or 'well done mate.' He was all a bit cynical saying it's not what it's cracked up to be and 'how can I know her after a few weekend passes' and saying that it's because it is wartime and it'll be different when the war's over. When I said we'd set a date for the first weekend in July, it almost seemed as if he didn't want me to be happy no matter what I did. It was a bit peculiar. He sort of perked up a bit though when the conversation got back on to the camp and work etc. and after another pint he was alright. Things continued Ok for a week or so until myself and a few others found our names on a list for an Anti Gas Course, on the camp.

It was to be in two parts, one in a classroom and the other on an outside area. There were about twenty of us, the armourers that were available, a few of the military police and some army NCOs. The instructor started by telling us that Germany was now finding it difficult to be fighting a war and as they got more desperate to get the advantage, they really meant to beat us. He said they would use more desperate techniques and one of these could well include the use of toxic gas and 'blister agents' which could be a gas or a very fine powder. The gas been used in the first world war twenty-five years ago so they may well use it again but this time they had the means to drop any amount on the British Isles. He went on to point out that Britain could never be 'gassed' into submission but any use of gas would cause fear and panic and create a great amount of disruption. This was quite worrying stuff as most people had heard of mustard gas being used in the trenches in the first world war but it had been relatively local to the field of conflict. What we were hearing now was that quite literally out of the blue, our population might be attacked with gas maybe at any time. He was then describing the various types of gas mask and how they worked with charcoal impregnated with chemicals that neutralised the gas. He continued to explain there was a sort of oil skin type of suit that resisted any gas penetration and there was an Anti Gas Ointment that you could rub on skin or clothing to give protection. We were told that we would be issued the 'suites' should the need arise! He also told us if anyone became contaminated for any reason they should be thoroughly doused with copious amounts of water to neutralise the agents. The other part of the instruction was to do with the duties of service personnel should the camp come under a 'gas' attack. The agents of the gas would settle over the camp, the equipment and the aircraft making them unusable so part of our duties would be to decontaminate the area and equipment with 'anti-gas powder' made up from hydrated lime and bleaching powder. The instructor didn't specify just how we were to do it though. I thought that with all the ground equipment on site let alone the areas involved, the task, if it came to it, would be monumental. I soon smiled to myself when I remembered the equipment I'd seen on the farms when I'd been 'dealing' with the petrol. On a couple of the farms I'd seen new equipment that was used for spraying fertilizer or something over the fields. I decided there and then that if I was involved in that sort of job, it was that type of equipment I would requisition from the farmers roundabout us. As it happened though, the anti-gas powder got the first 'strike,' in a minor sort of way. A stock of the powder had recently been delivered and was already on camp near the armoury and two of us were detailed to move it to a stock area. It seemed a straight forward sort of job. There were a few 1 cwt. drums of powder to move under cover. We started OK and easily managed to roll them on one edge but whether I lost the balance of mine a bit or missed my footing or something, the other lad couldn't help but knock the 'drum' I was moving and in an instant mine had rolled right over my foot causing me severe pain! It really did hurt like hell. So, with the other lad helping me we hobbled our way over to sick quarters for someone to have a look at it. After a few ums and ahhs by the medic, I was diagnosed with a broken toe. Eventually I got back to the armoury and reported in. There was nothing anybody could do about it but it was such a minor injury it was embarrassing and I did get the 'mickey' taken out of me as a result. The Officer in Charge though did have a much more practical approach to my predicament as he ordered a couple of the others to bring my bed and bedding to the armoury so I could continue the work I was doing. This was a bit of a tall order as I was billeted on the satellite camp. Eventually another bed and bedding was procured and I became the first ever full time resident in the armoury. This lasted until I could walk which I could do if I was very careful after about a week or so but it hurt for a long time afterwards. June soon passed with mum and dad making arrangements for the wedding. July saw me with not only a 48 hours pass but when the Officer I/C understood my reason; he was good enough to let me travel up to Manchester on the Friday. I really appreciated that as it gave me almost an extra day so to speak and I did thank him for it.

That weekend really flew by as I'd barely got through the door and my mum was on about getting things washed and pressed. She was telling me all the arrangements that had been made and who was doing what and when. It was a relief when Llewellyn and me went for a drink later on Friday night. We had a good chat and I felt a lot better about things afterwards. We weren't going to have a honeymoon and on Saturday night Elsie and myself were staying at my mum and dads. Everything did go very well though with Llewellyn as Best Man, myself and all our family filling the first three rows. Mum and dad had gone to a lot of effort to make a really nice spread at the reception. A little problem was further compounded as now there were three Mrs.

Butterworths within a few 'doors' of each other. By Sunday evening, after so much tea and all the pleasantries being observed throughout the day, I was soon back in the Hillman driving back to Kidlington feeling rather pleased with myself.

    I got back early evening feeling pretty tired but basically quite pleased with things. I was sat on my bed just sorting a few things out when in came Brian. I don't know if he'd already had a drink but he wanted 'us' to go for a drink and have a few pints to celebrate etc. He was very enthusiastic about it and really very persistent but I hadn't had anything to eat and was ready to turn in really. Brian did eventually go away but he was mumbling something about not being a very good 'sport.' It was about an hour and a half later that he returned, just before 'lights out' and he was just about legless. He came over and sat on my bed. Although he had a skinful he didn't seem too bad but a bit cynical, going on about mates sticking together and things like that. A few weeks earlier, I'd being given a Commando knife from the paratrooper lot and Brian knew this as he had been given one some time earlier and he knew I kept it handy under my pillow. He was still sort of chatting when suddenly he leaned over and got my knife out. Now these sort of things were 'key' possessions and certainly private property and for anyone to take it let alone without asking was very much 'crossing the line.' Pissed or not, Brian knew this as well but then the prat started fooling around with it. I was quite annoyed and got up sharpish and demanded he return it. Brian turned to me and really aggressively lunged at me with the knife. I caught his 'knife hand' as I side stepped and he went to my side but that swung me round on to his free hand which was about to 'land one' on me. I grabbed hold of it and held it as tight as I could. As he turned towards me, he was actually smiling. I could keep his 'knife hand' away from me but he brought it up in an arch towards my face. I certainly wasn't going to have any of that and then drove his hand across between us. There wasn't a lot of control being exercised and the force of diverting the knife away pushed it straight into his forearm. It certainly halted matters instantly and he did stop smiling. I didn't feel too bad about the pain when I pulled the knife out. Brian was instantly then occupied with gripping his left forearm and trying to stop the flow of blood! I cleaned the knife and put it back. He was swearing blue thunder at me but I still managed to tell him to go to sick quarters and get it looked at. He left but he was really annoyed but even now I'm not sure why. For all I knew he had gone over to camp sick quarters so I was a bit surprised when he turned up again about half an hour later. Apparently he had called at a transport cafe about seventy yards away and they had bandaged it for him. He was a lot better though and kept apologizing. He invited me to his bunk for a drink to sort of 'make up' for behaving like a fool. I didn't want to go but I did so to humour him if nothing else. As we went in to his room he was in front and anyone behind including me wouldn't see past him. So we had just gone in to his small bunk room when he reached forwards, out of my view as I was behind him, into the corner and turned round to present me with the very wrong end of a double barrelled shot gun. With his cynical grin he told me to 'now try it.' It wasn't a time for thinking too much. I figured that he wanted me to plead my case and talk my way out of it but he was pissed and I wasn't. The thing he least expected me to do was to not say anything and just 'go for it.' So that's what I did. I twisted round to one side and just grabbed the gun to direct it away. It didn't take too much to wrestle it from him as his left arm wasn't too good. I then reversed direction and cracked him across the head with butt enough to lay him out, then broke the gun, ejected the cartridges and locked him in his bunk. I was really pissed off by now as well as being dead tired so I went over to the same transport cafe and phoned the guardroom and explained what had happened and left it up to them.

The following morning as soon as I got to work I was told to report to Station Headquarters. I had expected that as they would want a formal explanation of events so off I went. As I went in a military police was there who 'escorted' me to the Commanding Officer's office. I expected this as well but the floor could have opened up and swallowed me at what I heard next. It was only myself that was to be charged with grievous bodily harm and malicious intent! At first I just couldn't comprehend it, then as both 'versions' of the incident were recounted it was plainly obvious that Brian's version of the account was completely fabricated as he'd used the fact he was a corporal to lie and discredit me by making out he was sober and that it was my knife that stabbed him to put the whole blame on me. Initially Brian was charged with affray and unreasonable conduct but ended up wriggling out of it and only got reprimanded. For myself, my charges were found proven and I was ordered to move back to the main camp accommodation and got fourteen days jankers for good measure. I was livid, but couldn't do anything about it. Again, I was blamed and the other sod, the real culprit was let off. I could see how this 'justice' worked. After my two weeks of Jankers, I applied for an overseas posting again. Even though I'd just got married, the war was going to keep me occupied whether I was at 'home' or abroad and I was feeling really cheesed off with the Sayle incident, almost as if I had been betrayed. Things were fine with Elsie and Mary but I just wanted a change of scenery. Work at the armoury was pretty constant, I was still doing some of the projects and the exercises still took place but I only ever spoke to Brian when I had to. About four weeks after my jankers had finished, I had a 48 hours pass and made a point of having a pleasant weekend at home with Elsie and the family. I'd written a couple of letters in-between times and it did feel pretty good to greet Mrs. Butterworth, Elsie, my wife. Even though we were both still at mum and dads, there was a lovely homely feel to the place and it was just nice to be there. Privacy was in rather short supply but neither of us minded too much. It seemed that all of Saturday I was being brought up to date with who was doing what, what had happened and more importantly what hadn't happened. It was all a nice change apart from the food rationing, which was always highlighted at mealtimes. But, luck was to dump a rather large fly in my rather nice bowl of ointment. It came in the form of a telegram delivered by a young Post Office lad just after tea. I had to sign for it and then read it. It requested my immediate return to camp. I was wondering about it for a while, thinking carefully as I was certain I hadn't been involved in anything for a few weeks, then, I concluded that it must be about the posting application I'd made. Everyone was concerned and disappointed, including myself but what was done, was done and now I'd have to follow it through. At six o'clock in the evening though even if I set off straight away I may well not reach camp that night so it'd probably be best to start early tomorrow morning. Then there was my car to think about as if I was getting posted even maybe abroad, I didn't want it sitting around some car park for months on end so Llewellyn offered to come down with me and bring the car back in any case. That seemed a good idea.

On Sunday morning, after a bit of breakfast, I got hold of what petrol I could and we set off for Kidlington, about 120 miles away. My thinking had been right as when I got to the guardroom and reported in I was told of my posting and that I had a berth booked on RMS *Andes* sailing from West Kirkby Liverpool on 27 August. I was glad there was Llewellyn to see me off, so to speak and we said our goodbyes. I had to get my clearance chit 'signed up' immediately though. A few weeks ago that would have been quite easy but recently the 3rd Airborne Division had been moved to Shobdon near Hereford and I now had to get my chit signed by them. There was nothing simple. As they had recently moved there was still quite a bit of traffic to Kidlington so the Officer I/C the armoury made a couple of phone calls then told me to get down to dispersal where I could board a Hotspur glider to fly me to Shobdon about a one hour trip. I got the clearance signatures I needed then flew back. A most fruitless record breaking attempt if ever there was one! After that, I collected the rest of my kit then with a travel warrant got a train up to Liverpool, heading for RMS *Andes*.

CHAPTER TEN
Down the Cape

I got to West Kirkby alright and I reported in OK. There were a lot of big ships throughout the docks and although it was quite busy, I expected to find a lot more people milling about. I was told the ship I was to board and where to find it. I was also told it wasn't going to sail for another two days, so that answered why the place wasn't as busy as it might be. I was a bit annoyed but that only turned to dismay when I found the 'transit' accommodation that I was allocated, along with thirty others, was a very neglected looking brick dormitory building, plain and depressing. We all spent two days awaiting embarkation in miserable spartan accommodation but the 29 August came and with around 6,000 other good souls I boarded the Royal Mail Ship *Andes*. I collected my boarding pass as I eventually went aboard amongst hundreds of other personnel all with coats and bags just everywhere. I found I'd been allocated to 'F' deck which turned out to be just about at the plimsoll line. I thought at the time that if we did get any torpedo attacks, it would be all or nothing at this level. Everywhere had the same sort of look, heavy steel floors, steel walls and steps and rails and it was always hard cold and usually grey. There were two large cabins which accommodated our draft of 168 men. There was no question of any personal 'space' and I didn't want to think about any sleeping arrangements so I satisfied myself that I knew where I had to come back to and went up on deck to see what there was. There were just men everywhere. There were still hundreds queuing along the dock shuffling along and waiting to board. There were hundreds already on the ship and most of them, like me had come up on deck to see what was going on. This continued for a couple of hours but then the queues got shorter and then finished. It seemed to take ages but slowly gangway by gangway and rope by rope we gradually became isolated from the dock. Almost in perceptively, the narrow band of water between us and the dock slowly got wider. You couldn't hear it more like feel it as a deep throbbing resonance developed. The band of water now grew in width, we were underway. That was it. That was the most exciting part over with. From now on, we the 6,000 had nothing but our own devices to look forward to for the next four weeks. The exception to that would be possible attacks from packs of U boats, but nobody wanted to think about that. The *Andes* turned out to be quite a large ship at 29,000 tons and I was told 'she' (as I found out that all ships are called) was fast enough to be able to travel alone as she could out run the German U boats. The fact we were travelling in convoy eliminated that possibility, but it was nice to know that she could. Gradually people started moving around and grouping together, some went below while loads of us filled the gangways to watch our beloved England get left behind. Initially we were going from Liverpool up to the Clyde in Scotland to meet up with the rest of our convoy which was WS 22 then head out for Iceland. Overall there was to be about twenty merchantmen en route with an escort of about seven or eight Royal Navy ships. Sometime before we got to Iceland we turned west so that we were headed for the USA. This peculiar route wasn't random as we were following the established convoy shipping routes to give the U boats as wide a berth as possible. As evening encroached and hunger, more people made their way to their designated accommodation area. They would normally be called cabins but 'cabin' was for too grand a name for what we had. 'Cabins' was what they were called when there was only the normal 650 fare paying passengers on board. What we had were very large metal rooms with fixed long, steel mess tables and benches which accommodated about ten men each side. At meal times the end two people of each table went to the galley to get the meals for all the people on their table. It seemed to work fairly well but if something was popular on the menu there were often arguments about the size of portions! On one side of the 'room' all the hammocks were stowed away. Sometime before lights out the hammocks were all strung up across the fixed mess tables. It was very cramped and always hot and stuffy but it did work. There were some serious complaints from anyone who fell out of a hammock though. In the mornings, the hammocks were stowed away, then there was 'reveille,' then communal ablutions were undertaken, then breakfast took place.

 The following day we turned to a more southerly direction to take us down the West Coast of Africa towards Freetown. It was always very blustery on deck and there was a fair swell but I thanked my lucky stars I was travelling in September rather than the winter. I'd seen on some newsreels how unforgiving and turbulent the sea can be and I had no wish to experience bad weather. In no time at all though necessity ironed out a routine for everyone but those first two or three days were a nightmare as it took 6,000 troops quite a while to find where everything was. But things changed as well, nothing to do with the layout of the ship or the daily routine or anything like that. With about 12 hours a day to kill, on average, the men created their own past times. Within a couple of days several different barbers were known about throughout the ship and even if you didn't really want a hair cut, the time that was spent in the queue used up that excess of time. It wasn't just waiting either because you would always end up chatting to somebody who was waiting in the queue as well. Tombola schools sprang up and many questionable games of 'housey housey' and as it was a large ship these were often duplicated through different deck levels and front to back (fore to aft). Card schools were all over the place and human nature being what it is these usually drew quite an audience. Another popular option was fishing. There was an amazing diversity of hooks and line that came from amazing sources. The favourite bait was bacon rind and I did actually witness a few people catch a fish. As so many of these activities got established there then became another alternative of visiting the various areas of activity just out of curiosity. A certain amount of time could be spent each day having a shower. It was a saltwater shower using crude lumps of 'superfatted' soap, but a daily shower still absorbed some of that killer time. A further option that endless people succumbed to was watching the sea, assessing the weather, debating our true direction or speed or load or nearly anything. I had a go at a few things, but mostly I was a traveller, wandering very slowly from one group to another. I enjoyed looking out to sea, knowing that I was travelling across the world and often imagining where I was going. Somewhere within all this inventive occupation I ended up talking to all sorts of people from all of the services and from all over Great Britain. There were so many men you could get lost in them but for all of that, I ended up chatting with a chap called Ian Wainwright. He was a similar age and he was an Armourer in the RAF but more surprising, he was in our draft. That was a few days in to the voyage and we quickly became good mates. Like anyone might do that has a burden of time to kill almost anything was discussed and all the basics were covered like where you lived, your last job, family etc. and what you'd done and what you could brag about. There was an amazing amount of knowledge divulged and almost just as quickly forgotten by the recipients.

When I came across Mac, I thought he was already a mate of Ian's but really but he had only mentioned him as another armourer. Anyway we were then three armourers together and even though he was Scottish he basically stuck with us and eventually went through the usual conversations. One of the few highpoints of the trip was the news of the Australians success in taking Madagascar.

On the 9 September we saw the harbour of Freetown in front of us. It was enormous and looked as though it needed to be as there were just loads of ships there, and big ones at that. Some were berthed at the docks while some were being re-supplied in the harbour enclosure as the make up of the convoy changed depending on who or what was going where. All we got was more intense boredom. It was bad enough having sod all to do while you were actually travelling somewhere but to be stationary as well was somewhat testing! On the third day, the 13 September things changed and we got under way for Capetown only seven days away with an escort of eight naval ships.

On 25 September we finally steamed in to Table Bay which was overlooked by the famous Table Mountain. After what seemed like an age it was our turn to enter the enormous harbour and berth. There was certainly no reluctance to disembark. All of our draft and most of the other drafts were destined for a transit camp called Pollsmoor about twenty miles south east of Capetown. That was all the information we were given and with our rail passes, that was where we had to get to. There were a few lads that talked about just getting 'lost' in Capetown but with no contacts, no information and no money it didn't seem an idea to be entertained in my eyes.

After a lot of messing about, myself and a few hundred other personnel boarded a train which eventually arrived at a nondescript station in the middle of nowhere with sandy scrub and tufts of couch grass here and there. It was a bit like being at a theatre really because as the full curtain of the train departed down the lines, it left us all to be presented with the stage of tens of acres, covered with hundreds of

THE CAPE PENINSULA

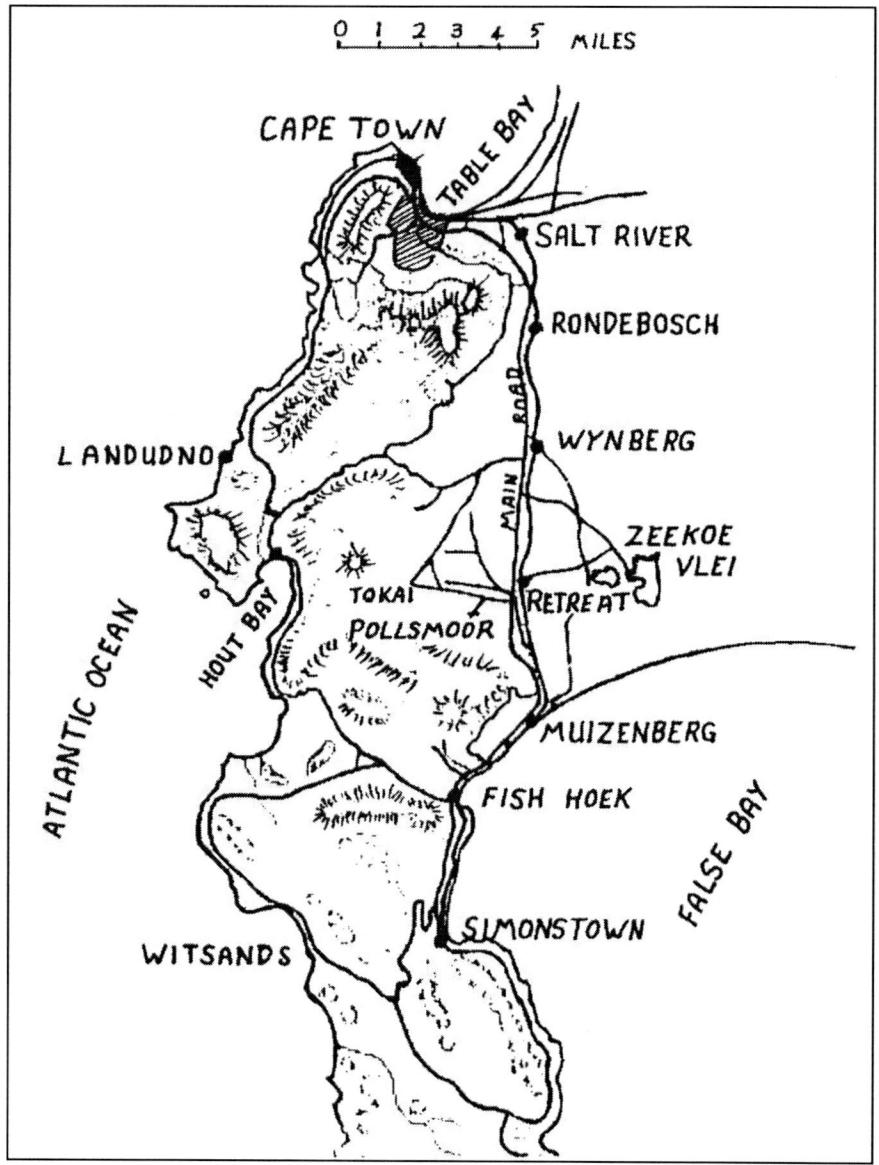

3. Location of Pollsmoor in 1942

army bell tents. Our new home at Transit Camp Pollsmoor. For all the huge number of tents that were there, our arrival seemed pretty straight forward. Every arrival got issued a tent number and block. Ian, Mac and me had managed to keep together and got the same number and block. From all the hundreds of tents, it was really easy to find even with the bit of a hike that was involved to get there. All the tents had been erected in regular blocks and lines so we only had to count five blocks east and three blocks north and then our number, to lead us to our summer retreat! Breakfast was available if you got to the mess tent early enough otherwise the evening meal was at half hour sittings, 17:00 hrs. to 18:00 hrs. but the room service was terrible! There was a movements tent with notice boards erected where the daily movement list of personnel was posted. The only essential thing we had to do every day was to check if our names were on the list, and be available for roll call. That might have seemed a pretty cushy number at first but we quickly realized we had no idea where we were really or where anything else was. No one had much money, we didn't know where to go or how to get there and there was no one to tell us what to do but apart from all that, we could do what we liked! We agreed to meet up at dinner and pool what we had found out. A few lads had organised some ball games on the edge of camp but after being cooped up on board for a month, I was interested in travelling somewhere, anywhere! I made a bee line for the staff on the control gate. I figured they must have been here at least some sort of time so should know what's about and how far it is. There was a small town nearby called Retreat but they didn't advise that as it was overrun with servicemen! The favourite was a small coastal town called Muizenberg. It was a four mile walk south and there was a servicemen's club more or less on the beach where most people went sooner or later so it was a good place to find things out. Other than that, it was a twenty mile train ride to Capetown or a hike in the bondu. The choice was ours!

Having lived cheek by jowl with a few thousand blokes for so long, we were all yearning for a bit of civilisation and normality. Capetown to the north seemed to be the place. We would get the train there and have a good view of the countryside in-between the towns we passed through such as Plumstead, Kenilworth, Mowbray and Zoute (means salt river). Capetown was another experience altogether. All the streets were wide with street lights that actually came on when it was dark, unlike the blackouts at home. The weather was glorious, all the shops were open and the people all seemed quite friendly. Just the smells along the street were refreshing with the sweet shops, the grocer's shops, and the smell of food and coffee from the cafés. There were plenty of bars open with no restrictions and what with the harbour and port in the town it was almost like being on holiday.

After a few trips to Cape Town I got nicknamed 'Commando Kenny' after the Commando Whiskey that I used to drink. It wasn't really special but it was popular, fairly cheap and it worked! But the Australians were the best at celebrating as was proven when we were there sometime in November. The newspapers were full of reports of Madagascar being surrendered to the allies from Vichy France and many of the Aussies were taking leave. They saw fit to celebrate for some days and became remembered as the 'wild Aussies.' On one occasion they thought it a good idea to deposit an Austin 7 in a hotel doorway and another time they overturned a brewers horse dray, broached the barrels and drank the beer in the street. I didn't want to enjoy myself as much as that. Occasionally two or three of us would go to the cinema and have a meal or sometimes go out and about sightseeing, sometimes to a beauty spot at Camps Bay which was a beautiful place with a cafe and people to meet. There always seemed to be something to do. A fair number of lads went to considerable lengths to engage with the local girls, with varying success. In the City Hall dances were held quite regularly as a means of entertaining the allied forces which were pretty good. Being a bit of a rural lad though, I felt a bit awkward about it all as I hadn't been married six months and I did miss Elsie really, and belonging and having a home, I guess.

My real favourite was walking to Muizenberg about four miles away, quite often with Mac and Ian even if their company was so predictable. In the morning the air was fresh, it was warm and pleasant and we were on solid dry ground and not far from the coast. The area around was sandy scrub to start with but as we got nearer the town there were farms or plantations of probably fruit trees and the like. As we dropped down and approached the town it reminded me of Morecambe but not as big. The town sat within a large curved bay with beaches and a sea front promenade along it with all sorts of shops and cafes and people strolling around as though they were on holiday. To one end we saw the building of the servicemen's club as described, more or less on the beach with the footings in the sea. As we went in it was like a large cafe really. It was run by the WRVS and it felt very comfortable with pictures on the wall with tables and chairs near the servery and to one side some easy chairs near the windows. There was a warming smell of coffee and fresh baking. The place didn't appear fantastic in any way but it did feel very comfortable, maybe a little homely. We all liked it straight away and approached the counter to our left with a glass cabinet and crockery stacked either side of the serving area. A young woman was behind the counter with her back to us initially and there were two other ladies sorting out the tables. As ours heard us she turned around. It was like another presence had arrived. She was bright, pleasant, she was smiling, was quite attractive and just exuded personality. Whoever owned the establishment was most astute. She straightened her apron around a slim waist.

'Hiya chaps, come on in. What can I get you this morning?'

She was scanning all three of us but seemed to dwell on me a little.

'We've got everything you can see.' she said, waiting for an answer. We were looking but I was seeing lovely dark brown eyes above a pert yet straight nose set against a fair complexion with freckles. Mac asked her something about what juice they had. As she turned around her long dark hair shimmered through the sunlight from the window. As she turned back she jokingly called me Captain which caught me off guard as I was then looking straight into her eyes. My mind just went blank as I tried to fathom the hidden depths. It was only a few moments but thank god for Ian who saved my embarrassment by lightheartedly admonishing the girl by declaring, 'He's no captain. That's Commando Kenny.'

'Gosh.' she exclaimed. 'You really a commando then?'

I didn't have time to answer as Mac was quick off the mark as well.

'Commando? Pull the other one love. The only thing commando about Kenny is the whiskey he drinks.'

She rolled her eyes slightly.

'Well we ain't got any of that here. So what you having?'

I'm not sure if I said a tea because I preferred one or because it would take her longer to make it. I was quite disappointed when she told us to 'get a table' and she would bring the drinks over to us.

I hesitated while Ian and Mac moved away then leaned over and asked her what she was called.

'Well, that would be telling now, wouldn't it?' she smiled. As if willed by god himself, a miracle then took place as a course dominant voice carried from across the room.

'Valerie! Less chatting!'

Now it was my turn to smile.

We got to like Muizenberg very quickly and often frequented the town and the club. I sometimes visited on my own as I found the comfortable atmosphere most conducive for writing letters home, as did so many other servicemen. Although Valerie at the Servicemen's Club was really pleasant and friendly I think it was the comfortable atmosphere about the place that provoked thoughts of home and if I was wrong, I don't think I should be thinking about it. The point was that 'home' was a thousand miles away and I wasn't too sure just how good it was to dwell on the idea. This was a fantastic place but we were at war. All what was here was not permanent for us as we would soon be gone from here. To be sure, it did not pay to contemplate too much. There were always some options of things to do but always it either belonged to someone else or was somewhere else and after a while I felt I wasn't doing anything constructive but always just seeing something else. That's when I started looking around a bit more and found a couple of forces associations publicised that quite a number of locals welcomed servicemen by the offer of a meal or sociable visits and advice etc. After a brief enquiry I went to visit two retired school teachers on the out skirts of the town. Two sisters, Erica and Anna Colli Van Tomdor.

All the houses seemed really nice in the area, very clean with gardens and driveways. I took a taxi to the vicinity then walked a short distance to their house which looked like a bungalow with a large roof. I just knocked on the door and introduced myself.

'Good afternoon I'm Kenny Butterworth.'

'Ah, Kenneth, how do you do? Please come in.' I could feel myself wincing at being called 'Kenneth' but made a determined effort not to show it. I was only ever called that by my mother when I was getting a telling off.

'I'm Anna and just through there, is Erica.' I was directed into a large pleasant sitting room.

Anna was an older lady that looked very pleasant and dressed well probably for their surprise guest but although she spoke English it sounded like she was foreign. I hadn't spoken to many South Africans so I wondered if that is what South African sounded like. I suppose it was. We went through to a drawing room where Erica was sat. I reckoned she was a little shorter than Anna and carried a little more weight but was equally pleasant.

'Erica, this is Kenneth.'

'Well hello Kenneth, do come in and sit down.' I sat down in a very comfortable chair that was offered.

'Can we get you a tea, lemonade or juice?'

'Lemonade will be fine, thanks.' Anna, who was waiting for the 'order' came back with three lemonades, served them and sat with us. 'I suppose all of this might first seem a little strange' Erica said. 'And it is not our routine to invite gentlemen to visit, but if we can help our troops get the upper hand in any way, then it's on.' They both smiled to each other.

'And I can tell you that it's much appreciated Erica. It's really nice to have the pleasure of a bit of company in such a nice place.'

'We know this is no substitute for your home, but it probably gives you a bit of a change.' It certainly did, it had a warm feeling about the place, homely with a sense of belonging. I think it was to save a little awkwardness that at first they told me some of their background. How they had both been teachers in Cape Town since they moved south at the end of the Great War. Before that they had both lived a few miles from Freetown but their father had been in the Boer conflict at the turn of the century, so both of them had experience of 'troubles.'

'But that's nothing to the like of what that upstart Hitler's playing at.' Continued Erica.

'He's no right to force all those young men to fight and needs to be stopped.' Anna and I both agreed.

Anna was quick to start 'Kenneth. Tell us a bit about yourself. Where do you come from? Have you got any family?'

'Err, right. Well there's me, mum and dad and Llewellyn my brother. He's three years older. We used to live in Salford, but about six years ago we moved to Swinton, 91 Folly Lane. It's about two miles from Swinton, in the countryside really. In the other direction is Eccles with Manchester five miles away.'

'Oh, we've heard of Manchester.' said Anna.

'And your parents?' Erica enquired.

'Well, my mother, she's just a good mum. She's a great cook because she used to be a pastry cook at Bailey's in town. Her apple pies are brilliant and we have, well used to, really nice roast dinners at the weekend.'

'It sounds like you're a very fortunate lad, Kenneth. What about your brother Llewellyn?' asked Anna.

'Oh, Llewi's alright. When we were younger we used to play together, especially among the fields and riverbank behind our house but he is a bit more serious than me and as we got older we just got different friends.' The lemonade I had was really good.

'He got married a couple of years ago and now his wife's sister Elsie is my wife.'

'It sounds like you've got a close community. And what about your father? He sounds like someone special.' prompted Erica.

'Well we mum, Llewi and myself, think he is.'

I suppose it was only with hard experience of the real world that I had fully come to appreciate the endeavours of my father. At an early age he had impressed me with his presence and strength of character and continued to do so. My father was about 5' 8" and of quite a heavy build. He had worked on the railways some where in Africa for twenty years, mostly as a foreman Plate Layer. He used to spend eighteen months out there, have five months holiday with two weeks travelling each way, which made a very unorthodox lifestyle for a working man. So my first memory of meeting my father was at three years old, being scooped up in powerful arms and drowned in affection by quite a burly gentleman whilst being tickled by a generous moustache and neat beard. I remember my mother and brother Llewelyn, receiving very similar treatment. With a full head of hair, he always seemed remarkably full of life and very healthy. Later on I realised that this was in stark contrast to his working circumstances, as the 'gold and ivory coast' of West Africa was known as the 'white man's grave,' due to the diseases that killed so many Europeans. He was a good survivor, but like all the others, he did succumb.

As soon as Africa was mentioned their faces lit up somewhat.

'My word. What an exciting life.' said Anna 'But where was he working?' she continued.

'He never said exactly, only the 'gold and ivory coast'.' I paused as in deep thought. I continued, 'The only thing that might be a clue,' I said, 'is that when we moved to our new house, after he'd retired, he called it 'Kaduna."

'Really!' Erica's face lit up. 'Anna. You remember cousin Pietor, from up north. He's mentioned Kaduna!'

'That's right. It's a large river.' There then followed almost a period of excitement as they committed themselves to finding out about Kaduna from several gazetteers. They did find quite a bit out as well. It appeared that for years now a railway had been under construction through the jungle, heading inland and more or less following the course of the River Kaduna from Lagos heading north east inland about 550 to 600 miles. Also further south another railway was under construction northwards from Port Harcourt and these both converged at a place now called Kaduna. I guess my dad had been working on the railway and had named our house after the new town. I could see a connection but there wouldn't be many people who know that. Certainly not in Swinton.

I told them they needn't have gone to so much trouble but they said they enjoyed being able to help.

'It's really nice to have a bit of company in a real home.' I said.

'Well it's the least we can do.' replied Anna. Well it wasn't the least they could do at all as I was soon shown through to the smaller dining room where I was presented with a prepared table with a large bowl of lush green salad with plates of sliced chicken and ham and dishes of chutneys and beetroot. It was thoroughly enjoyable and the dessert, although I wasn't too sure just what was in it, was equally good. As the time came for me to leave, so ended quite a memorable and remarkably pleasant day.

The next three or four weeks were just an assortment of ways to kill some time and find things to do. It wasn't any hardship and there are thousands that would have swapped places with us in a trice but after four weeks we were all getting 'itchy feet.' All things changed the day we saw our names on the notice board in a draft destined for Durban. Geographically it was on our way to India as it was a few hundred miles further around the coast but it was still on the wrong side of the Indian Ocean and a very long way from India. After talking to so many of the other lads we were a bit more familiar with movements now and Ian, Mac and myself with about three hundred other lads found ourselves at the docks in Capetown waiting to board a ship. Eventually we started filing along to the dockside and up a gangway into our ship, the 10,000 ton *Ascanius*.

To call it a ship was certainly correct but the image that confronted us was far from 'ship shape.' It looked a wreck, a proper rust bucket. It was painted but on every other panel there were great stains of rust and from a distance it looked like a dirty grey ship turning bad with a mixture of red, brown and black patches all over. It had an open deck galley which supplied quite horrible food and was crewed by Lascas. It was a daunting thought to consider that this to be home for the next week. It was a dire thought that was only further endorsed by the fact that there weren't any mess decks because it was a steam freighter and had being damaged in WW1 and, as I found out, had more recently been condemned and used as a troop ship for Italian Prisoners Of War. But it was good enough to transport British troops! I, with many others had to sleep in the cargo hold with cock roaches and rats wandering about. On 'Boat Stations' which was a 'drill' for fire or attack, everybody had to be up on deck. When this occurred there wasn't an inch of spare deck to be seen, nor any order. The ship had a constant list all the way to Durban.

For everyone on board, we couldn't reach Durban soon enough but we did after seven days. And what a change Durban was. It was like being released from some dark horrible prison and being set in a clean thriving city and colourful. Everywhere there was colour, the trees, the houses, people's clothes and even the cars! The shops, cafes and bars all had colourful signs and the people were bright and pleasant and stopped for a chat. It was more tropical than Capetown with palm trees growing in the streets and on the market stalls there must have been every type of fruit known. We had travelled through a desert of oppression and gloom to arrive at an oasis of civilization and pleasantness. It cheered all of us up no end. The arrangements were similar to those at Capetown but here the Transit camp was only a few miles out of Durban. The Mess, dining hall could seat 2,000 men and the accommodation was brick built barrack blocks but still pretty basic though as we only had 'palliases' on the floor, a bit like straw filled mattresses to sleep on. As the town was within walking distance we often ended up being out in the town in the evening and what a spectacle it was. For the last eighteen months all of Great Britain had been living with the black out but over here in the evening the streets were vibrant with illuminated signs, neon signs, signs that flashed on and off and others of all colours. Doubtless the most attractive ones were over the bars but there were people and cars and taxi's all going about their business and enjoying themselves like I hadn't seen before and like there wasn't a war taking place at all. We could get a very nice mixed grill for 1s. 9d. and a bottle of Capetown Brandy for 6s. 6d. but even when we didn't have any money it was pleasant just to be there. But we weren't to have the pleasure for that long as after three weeks ours names were again on the movement's board for the *Sterling Castle* cruise liner to Bombay on 3 December. The whole operation of actually boarding the ship was quite routine now if not laborious but was completed without much ado. At this time though, there was a remarkable addition to the procedure which everyone noticed. On the dock side, stationed by the queues of troops waiting to board, there was a lady seemingly dressed in white with a broad rimmed hat. That in itself wasn't remarkable but she was singing in a loud sort of operatic voice really patriotic songs like *Land of Hope and Glory* and *Jerusalem*. It was no big deal, but I reckoned it was a really thoughtful sort of recognition to all serving troops. Once on board and loading was complete we got 'under way.' We still had three weeks of boredom to contend with but as the ship was less than seven years old we were bored in comparative luxury compared to the 'pits' of the *Ascanius*. After three weeks of beautiful sun, sea and total boredom we entered Bombay harbour to disembark on the 23 December.

CHAPTER ELEVEN

Dinner at the Palace

A group of us were going to sign in at Worli Camp where myself and a few others were posted to Jodhpur. None of us had heard of it or knew where it was but we did have a travel warrant to get there. On the way from the docks to the railway station it was amazing how so many of the big buildings were Victorian looking being made from brick and carved stonework, just like the cities in England. En route we passed the Towers of Silence which is a great archway formed by two large columns. At the very top there are steel bar grills which are open to the sky. I was told that the bodies of Parsees, a low Indian cast, are placed on grills and left to be eaten by the vultures, leaving the bones to fall down into a pit. It seemed peculiar but it was all to do with old religion.

Once at the railway station we found the platform for the train to Jodhpur which would stop at Delhi. It was only through chatting as we waited we realised Delhi is about 750 miles north of Bombay and Jodhpur is about 300 miles south east of Delhi. It was going to be quite a journey! In due course we were on our way and soon left the city and its suburbs behind and in no time at all the only countryside we were travelling through was scrub with a few hills here and there interspaced with an occasional bit of greenery. This continued for about three hundred miles or so.

Mile after mile of it. Slowly the scant bit of greenery reduced to just scrub and sand. We were entering the western side of the Great Thar Desert. Eventually though I realized I was getting impressed by the shear immense vastness of almost nothing. The only thing that actually changed after about a days travelling was our approach and stop at Delhi. The variety and confusion of the outskirts and the city was in total contrast to the previous hours of vast and monotonous scrub land. The passengers changed and we got inundated with local vendors of tea, chipatties, cakes and water. It looked like the engine was getting water and fuel before we set off again. As we set off the city was soon left behind and then the rural suburbs merged once again into semi-desert but not before I had noticed that some farmsteads seemed to have small fields in which appeared to grow large clay bells which totally bemused me. The farmsteads were quickly left behind to leave only the desert as our direction of travel changed to head south west for Jodhpur. After a couple of hours all the frustration of being so bored for so long just evaporated to a mind-numbing gaze at sand, rock and scrub flowing by mile after mile and hour after hour. This was unchanging for something like 5 hours or so. When we were still many miles from Jodhpur the response to the first indication that we were approaching the town woke everyone up. In the distance there seemed to be a large building on the horizon yet for quite a while it hardly grew any bigger. It did grow bigger, but only a little then it went out of sight as the track weaved its way between rocks and sand dunes. Sometime later it came into view again and now we could clearly see that it was some sort of castle or fort on top of a mountain. But how impressive, as we got closer we saw it was a huge fortress built right on top of a single mountain nearly half a mile long with a great outer wall all around the base. As we wearily approached there were settlements with tracks around then flat-roofed houses with goats and sheep in compounds and the clay bells. As we got closer it was evident that the town was sprawled around the southern area of the large outer wall at the base of the hill. The station was right in the middle of the town and could have come from any Victorian station in England. It was just three or four hundred yards from the vast outer walls of the Fort, as I found out later, the Mehrangarh Fort. As we got off the train it seemed as though this lovely very English looking railway station had been dropped in the middle of a large medieval town. As soon as we were out of the building everything became sandstone and clay lined walls of an infinite number of square looking buildings of every size with flat roofs. The smaller ones just had square holes for windows while the larger ones developed larger window shutters most of which were highly decorated. I don't know what the roads were made of but there was sand everywhere.

'Look. There's bloody cattle wandering around!'

'Bloody Hell, Ian. It looks like we've gone back in time, or something'.

'Well if we have, I hope it's a time that's got some sort of mechanized transport.' was Macs sombre contribution.

'Too true,' I joined. To be honest though I think we needed to find someone who was exceptionally philanthropic. I mean, we'd been in very basic accommodation in Durban for three weeks, been on a ship for another three weeks with only the most spartan of facilities available, then on a train all day in 90°F to 100°F with natives and sheep, goats and chickens and looked as though we'd just emerged from the centre of the earth. My money was on a long walk to camp.

'Come on. Let's look round for something.' Ian chimed, 'Camp can't be too far away'.

'I don't know about that, but let's go see then'.

We set off in the direction from where some sort of activity seemed to emanate, proceeding towards the base of the great outer wall. We reached what must be one of the main gateways into the old town enclosed on the other side of the wall. It was massive with fantastic stone work and carvings all around it and over the top. There was some movement of people and a few rickshaws but not what we had in mind and none really coming near us. As we stood there at the edge of a sort of square which lead to the gate entrance, waiting for inspiration, I noticed over the far side the end of a sign that was partially obscured. All I could see was 'bar'.

'Well I don't know about you but I know where I'm going'. That got their interest. I nodded, indicating across the square and immediately had committed followers. As we rounded a corner the sign grew to read 'Premvilla's Bar and Restaurant' and even more optimistically there was a couple of service trucks parked by it. We'd made it!

 The camp was about a mile and a half or so straight down the main road out of the town to the south. After what we all thought was the most beautiful beer ever, we got a lift to camp. Ian, Mac and myself arrived on Christmas Eve at 319 Maintenance Unit, Jodhpur and duly signed in. We went to find the 'Headquarters' and then to find a tent, just before dinner. To have some decent food and a good wash and a bed (space) that wasn't moving was a level of luxury that I'd forgotten about, and beautiful sleep.

The next morning I woke up and I was bloody freezing, I couldn't believe how cold it was. I couldn't see how a place that looked so dry and arid, with sand just like a desert could be so cold, but it certainly was! I got dressed and ventured outside. I still didn't know the right time but there was other activity around. It was sunrise, and how? Whatever the land was like, to the east basically was dead flat albeit with undulating sand dunes and scrub. I couldn't look directly at it but the sun was just sitting on the horizon and was a most intense vivid red but there was a band of brilliant red light hugging the entire curve of the horizon, just fading at the farthest limits. Just above the sun a transitional ribbon of watery greens and yellows quickly merged to the light blue of the sky. It was so impressive and weird as well because as it was so low everything was lit up completely from one side only and when I looked the other way it was like a huge flood light on the floor. I thought I'd seen some good sunrises in my time but this really took the biscuit. Of all the evolution and eternity that might be out there, for these few moments and my appreciation, time stood still.

The camp was basically the Maharaja's own aerodrome which had been commandeered by the RAF. It had one medium size hangar, work areas, some brick service buildings and some stone billets, a tailor, a NAAFI and Barber etc. The mess was quite adequate at about 25 ft wide and 65 ft long as there were only eighty-five to ninety airmen and about twenty Officers on camp in total. All the surrounding area was desert or semi-desert with a river looping round the far perimeter. A road ran through the camp and all the billets and accommodation was on one side, while the NAAFI, shops and tailor were on the other side, with an immaculate control tower all in white with some buildings, maybe offices on each side at ground level. Compared to what we were used to they stood out in a most pristine manner. There were a couple of generators and bowser's stood about and a few oil drums stacked against a wall. After visiting the mess my first job was to get some suitable 'kit' from the stores, then I'd find out what I was really supposed to be doing! I found the armoury 'area' and reported in. The Sergeant explained the general layout of the place and what our jobs were. He also asked me if I'd got my 'kit' ok, paused then added, 'and a new shirt? It's Christmas!' It seemed a bit unusual but I had a new shirt and so thought no more about it. He added that right now things were fairly quiet so I could take the rest of the day to settle in so to speak but to report back at 1600 hrs. Which is exactly what I did.

I got some breakfast and had a look around then wandered over to the hangar to see what was going on, but what a hangar! Overall it had two roof areas joined at an apex along the middle but the entrance was something else. On either side of the doors there were two vast columns higher than the roof with some sort of finial cum bust on the top and all very bright and pristine. The entrance to the airfield was all concrete which continued past the control tower and over to the hangar a little distance further on. The runway was a few hundred yards further across course sandy scrub, to the south. It was very quiet as they evidently didn't start too early, which seemed good to me. I entered the large doors of the hangar and had a look around which took a few seconds for my eyes to adjust from the brilliant sun outside. There were hoists, stands and trolleys for moving engines and the like with some benches and tool chests to one side. Then from nowhere this voice hollered.

'Butterworth! Get your arse over here!'

In a hangar it was difficult to tell where the noise came from and I was looking round for where I should be going to, quite sharpish. I just knew this bloke was a bastard. I wasn't doing anything wrong and there was no need for that shouting. I saw 'him' towards one corner and headed over. Something about him looked familiar.

As I got closer his voice was different as he said 'Now then, you old gyte. What did you do to get posted here?'

'What the bloody hell....? Ye gods.' Thousands of miles from 'home', I'd found my old mate Charlie Allen from Polebrook.

'I'm not really sure but I took the scenic route. Anyway, you must be doing alright (the three stripes on his arm said he was now a Sergeant). How the hell are you, and what's it like here?'

We had a chat and he told me how it was and what it was like and what we were supposed to do and all that stuff. He agreed that he'd been very lucky considering we'd all been charged together over the Ernie Jones incident. I was getting a good feeling for this place. For Christmas day, that wasn't bad.

As a Maintenance Unit, at any time we might have up to 250 aircraft stored on the dispersal area right on the other side of the airfield about a mile away. Some were there for a day while others were there for weeks including several larger bombers, like an aircraft poole. It depended why they were there, some were there because they were

4. The main hangar at the Aerodrome. Photograph taken by K. Wentzel in 1948. Copyright of National Geographic.

surplus to requirements at that time while others were there waiting for parts so they could be repaired. Our primary job was to remove all weapons from incoming aircraft for security and put the ammunition in safe custody. What with so many 'inspections' and different types of 'running repairs' as well, we were kept fairly busy. At this time there were a lot of tribal conflicts in the north of the country and the Pathana of the North West Frontier tribes would try to get guns and ammunition any way they could and likely as not use them on our lads. Hence all weapons and ammunition were removed and sent to a 'dump' at Jabalpur, at least a days train ride away, which was once a famous Victorian retreat for crocodile shooting.

'Right Kenny, I've got to get on.' he paused 'Make sure you're back here for 1600 hrs.'

'Yeah, sure, but what's going on?'

'You're going out to dinner Kenny.'

'Eh?'

'You, me and the whole bloody camp is going out for Christmas dinner!'

'How?'

'You see those white bits sticking up over there?'

'Yeah.'

'Well they're the tops of the domes on the Maharajas new Chittar Palace. We're going there.'

'Bloody hell.'

'Don't be late. I'll talk to you later.'

'OK Charlie, I'll see you later.' Then added 'Sergeant.' Charlie smiled.

Well, what would mum, or even dad come to think of it, make of this? I travel thousands of miles to a holiday camp, meet one of my best mates and then go for dinner in the Maharajas palace. What a life!

The state of Rajasthan occupies virtually all of the Thar desert which once encompassed a collection of princely kingdoms where feudal conflicts reigned amidst majestic palaces and rugged forts of stone in spectacular deserts and the occasional tranquil lake. Rajasthan is situated in the north western part of India. It covers about 140,000 sq. miles and the climate varies from arid to semi arid and although it is less harsh than similar countries the summers are dry and scorching and the landscape is generally parched, the exception being for a few weeks after the South West Monsoons in July. The temperature in the summer can be up to 48°C in places yet in the winter it can often drop to below freezing. The south eastern area over the Aravali Mountains is far more temperate with large fertile tracts. Jodhpur just north of them, once the capitol of the former princely state of Marwar, is flanked on its western side by the Mehrangarh Fort, sitting over 400 ft above the town and on its eastern side by the grand and stately, nearly completed, sandstone Chittar Palace on a hill about two miles away. The monuments, temples and gardens of Jodhpur collectively show an ancient mystical grandeur with customs that have transcended the centuries. The most outstanding of them due to its enormity and dominance is the Mehrangarh Fort. The ten kilometres of impenetrable outer walls around the base were the original defences of the town and the fort itself was large enough to accommodate all the temples required for continuity as well as the Royal Forces. It is only with the rate of natural progress and the proximity of the river that the town became developed around the southern section of the outer walls and the absence of conflict enabled the ruling Maharajas to build the splendid palaces and monuments. Only twenty years earlier in the light of technical developments, the Maharaja had his personal aerodrome built just to the south east of the town. At the outbreak of war the use of the airfield was offered to the Royal Air Force when more facilities were provided and the runway was extended to accommodate larger aircraft.

'Alright you lot! Fall into Line! Come on! Form three lines!' It was 1605 hrs and most of the camp personnel were assembled outside by the hangar and being addressed by the Duty Officer. 'Right, Turn. By the left, Quick. March!' Yes, we were marching to our Christmas dinner but it all seemed a fairly relaxed affair and I thought, in ignorance, that Kings Regulations didn't allow for the movement of troops any where without some form of marching being involved. The palace was just over half a mile away and all up hill. It was obvious there was something happening there as every few minutes en route there were cars or military vehicles and horse drawn buggies passing us. As we approached it though I couldn't imagine anyone not being impressed by the entire splendour of the whole building. It looked basically rectangular with a massive central dome for a roof and four sort of towers around it with ornate windows and carvings all around it but the whole thing had a sort of yellow sheen from the stone it was made out of. It must have been over two hundred yards wide with a fair depth to it and a front yard that was bigger than any as parade ground. We were halted a little distance from a flight of perfect stone steps that must have been a hundred feet wide that led to the grandest of front doors so to speak, then stood at ease. A Flight Sergeant presented himself but I was sure he hadn't marched up with us but he proceeded to address us. He told us that we were remarkably privileged to be such honoured guests of the Maharaja and informed us that we were representing the Royal Air Force and Great Britain by our presence and as such our conduct had better reflect that. It basically culminated with the instruction of 'You will like the food. You will conduct yourselves in a civil manner. You will, not, drink too much.' and 'You will enjoy yourselves. Is that understood? Company, Dismiss'. Uniformly, we all half turned, stamped a right boot and broke up. As a Flight we had arrived amongst groups of obviously important looking people from their dress. There were Colonial dignitaries, there were Indian Heads of State in ceremonial dress and medals shining all over the place and ladies in such remarkable dresses that I've never seen the like of and all of them seemingly guests of the afternoon garden party. There were a few quips being passed around about the guests but nobody was rushing for the door. Slowly, as a group we approached the immense doors. The first person entered followed progressively by the rest of us. I was somewhere in the middle and was impressed by being individually welcomed to the Chittar Palace of His Royal Highness the Maharaja of Jodhpur and wondered what his dedicated staff thought of repeating the same welcome so many times. If I was impressed by the welcome, that was nothing compared to the awesome grandeur of what was presented inside. The place was absolutely huge, whatever it was, pillars, windows, doors or stairs, but not only huge but perfect as well, flawless. Outside the entrance our assembled company of about seventy men had looked tiny yet our entrance to the palace was remarkably slow. As I entered and was welcomed I understood why. So many of our entry were stood just inside straining their necks upwards and sideways and back again dumbfounded at the size and splendour of the interior and the amazing domed roof. Everywhere was pristine stone and polished marble and it was so cool and scented. This was the entrance hall that was maybe forty feet high or more with small windows round the top and opposite the doorway across the floor was a three portal entrance over which was a balcony with the most impressive staircase anyone could see which curved equally down both sides of the room to an immaculately polished marble floor. It was difficult to take on board that it was real. This was the stuff we only ever saw pictures of, or on newsreels, but here we were, and for dinner! We fudged and shuffled along like confused sightseers through another large and elegant reception room and into what was called the Maplewood Ballroom. This was no less splendid than the entrance, just different. It had a very high ceiling, all decorated with polished stone columns along the walls with hanging drapes of some sort. The floor was all sort of chestnutty orange in colour and felt very solid and looked so perfect there was no trace of any gap in the woods at all. But how large it was! There were rows of prepared tables across the room but along one side was one table with the most lavish display of food that you could imagine. We paced it out before we were seated and it was fifty feet long and six feet wide and not only did it look small in the ballroom but it was loaded with an amazing selection of food. There were complete cooked and prepared pigs, all presented on their own platters, Black-bucks and deer with different breads and sweet meats. There were lavish dishes of whole fish and ducks all ornately decorated and trays of vegetables and greenery that some of which we didn't recognize and further bowls of fruits and nuts and chutneys. From the rations that everyone had been compelled to accept for so long and of the rationing that was in force at 'home', it seemed a miracle that such food could exist in front of us. As we were directed to be seated you could only imagine this is what the tables were like in the Ritz or the Waldorf maybe with the immaculate table cloths and the shiny cutlery and glasses with servings of pickles or sauces. I think the exception to the Ritz or the Waldorf though would have been the jugs of beer placed along the centre of the tables, except the top one where the officers were placed. I thought that was very thoughtful. We had to listen to a few words of welcome and appreciation of the

Maharajas hospitality from the CO then started about an hour and a half of bliss. There were so many courses and for some of them we had no idea about but how beautiful they were and to cap it all the jugs of beer were never left empty! Charlie (Sergeant) pointed out Flight Lieutenant Sutherland on another table who was our Armourment Officer and made a point of introducing me to some of the others. There were about seven or eight of us in our group. Les Morely had been evacuated from Java and Singapore, he was already at Jodhpur when I arrived. There was Ian Wainwright 'Chunky' was a really pleasant bloke, Danny Norm, Ted Orme and John Elliston, a Londoner. Everyone thought it was a brilliant meal and with so many different conversations we all really enjoyed it.

All of us were taken back to camp by Umaids troops in their trucks but 'some' stayed till very much later! All personnel that attended received an inscribed glass bottomed tankard and a Christmas card with a photograph of the Maharaja, from himself which were distributed by the Station Adjutant. The next day though it was a case of business as usual but not too many officers were available.

A large part of our job was done out on the dispersal area as the fitters did daily inspections etc and we fitted or removed weapons. One day a fitter opened the cockpit of a Vultee Vengeance to find a Viper on the cockpit seat. It's anyone's guess how long it had been there or how it got in there in the first place! As a Maintenance Unit all sorts of traffic arrived from all over the place or sometimes just refuelled and carried on their way. I had occasion to get chatting to a chap who'd just got back from the north of the country. He told me the area was called the North West Frontier and he'd been doing some survey work. The up shot of it was I bought a very nice 7.62 mm Berretta from him. He said that he'd been glad of it a few times and with different types of people around, it felt like a good idea. I was still well aware of the trouble I had got in to with the .38 pistol in Nottingham but this was a different situation and soon afterwards I did get a permit for it. He was only there until he got a lift to Bombay but we had a good chat as he was quite interesting. The only other thing that I got from him was something that will last for years. It was a phrase that he taught me. It was the first and only piece of 'Latin' I was to ever learn; 'nil desperandum illigitum carborundum', loosely translated as 'don't let the bastards grind you down!' How many times had I needed that sort of resilience?

Day to day operations took on some sort of regularity and we were usually out at dispersal working on the aircraft or we'd be in the armoury packing guns and ammunition up for transportation. Sometimes I managed to get a job where I was actually repairing something which I found more interesting. Wherever we worked we always kept an eye out for Tondrapani (Pani Walla), water man, used to come round with a goat skin of water and the 'char walla' (tea). We had a Pathani char walla, with baggy pants, who used to come round to the domestic site and dispersal, depending where we were working. We were fairly sure he was alright, but he could see the 'weapons work' as he wanted. He would have his tea urn in front of him, hung round his neck. The bottom part had small holes and a door in it, inside was a round dish with burning charcoal in it, it must have been a very hot weight. He would also carry cakes and lemonade which came in bottles closed by a rubber seal and a glass marble inside the neck. Tea and cakes was about 8 anna. There was a general sort of principal that you never paid cash for his wares, so it was always 'book John' indicating with a finger writing on ones palm that we wanted it written in his bill book. It was not uncommon for his 'customers' to erase their more expensive previous order and enter their 'cheaper' one. There was a serious point to this as although he did good business, he could quite easily earn enough to buy weapons and ammunition, which would find their way back to the North West Frontier and be used against our boys out there.

By and large I got on with all the lads alright and we soon figured out who liked doing what in our free time. Les Morley was a bit older than me and as he had been evacuated from Java and Singapore he was an 'old hand' as he had arrived when 319 MU was established here a few months earlier. John Eliston was a Londoner and we got on well. Everyone went into the town at some point or other but some more than others. Anti-British feeling was very strong in many areas of the city, and generally across the country and although Jodhpur was a lovely city to explore, we were we advised to be careful where we went and always to be in 'twos' or 'threes'. I used to go into town with John Elliston and Les Morely sometimes and at other times with Ian and

Mac from the boat. Most trips usually started with a walk into town to have a drink at Premvilla's where we'd decide on a route. From Premvilla's you looked out upon the Sojati gate, which was the main gateway to the old 'native' city parts that one had to walk through. Outside the city walls, was called the 'cantonments', inside the walls was the 'city' or 'native' city. Frequently a mate and I would go to the city, there were all sorts of everything there; animals, some tied up, some in cages and several that had been killed, so many different foods, fruits, fine materials, gold and jewellery. Our problem was that the nearer we got to a stall the higher the prices went, I remember a 6d. tube of MacLean's toothpaste cost me 1s. 6d. which was 4 rupees, once! Most of the lads adopted Premvilla's Restaurant and Bar, including myself, so with the extra custom, the prices were a little lower. Native whiskey 4 rupees/bottle, food was chapatti, a kind of pancake. Wherever you went they tasted different but by and large they were alright and they did make a change to what our Bobajee's, Indian cooks, served up.

Ian Wainwright was a really nice chap with a stocky sort of build and he just ended up with the nickname of 'Chunky'. We sometimes hired a couple of horses and went riding around the camp. It was 1 Rupee for a horse for an hour or so. We'd go around the edge of the camp which was about two and half miles. It was very peaceful being out in such a vast open space and there were the different aircraft to 'mull' over and we had a good few chats about home life and all sorts of things. Sometimes we'd see a bit of wildlife with the odd snake or stray goat. Les had told me there wild dogs roaming around, a bit like dingos and they were always half starved and scavenging for food. They were quite vicious, so to give them 'a wide berth'. He said a friend of his, a local chap called Josh told him that recently some hunters in the town had shot wild boar and cougars in the hills not far away. Another far less obvious problem apart from the scorpions, spiders and snakes was disease. You couldn't be sure of the local water or produce really and malaria was a common occurrence.

At the domestic site our billets were not bad overall and quite comfortable apart from the incessant heat and, of course the sand and a few uninvited guests which crawled in. Quite a number of local people were employed in various jobs like the tondrapani, with the water and we had a moochi walla, as a cobbler. We had a nappi walla for a shave and a beasti walla as our sweeper up. We also had a bearer named Clancy. Les told me about not tipping him too much for similar reasons to our char walla. He was as black as coal but he was on such a 'good number', he earned more than me! He had four billets to look after with twenty men in a billet. We paid him 1 rupee each, so he earned 80 rupees a week'. 1 rupee was about 1s 6d with about 13 ¼ rupees to the pound. My wage as Corporal group 2 Armourer was 35 rupees/fortnight. The wage for bearers or coolies was 16 rupees/month, so Clancy was 'bloody rich' by comparison and sometimes got a little too big for his boots. If he got a bit 'stroppy', Danny Norm or I would give him a belt across the backside, just to remind him. For all that the native Indians used to prattle on about, as there were so many visiting staff all the time they were often a good means of finding out local gossip and quite often, spreading rumours as required. Our tondrapani (pani walla), water man was most proficient. Most times I wouldn't give two hoots for what he had to say but today his news sounded quite definite. He was telling us that in about a weeks time on the 14 February there was going to be the biggest celebration ever known in the town. The eldest son and royal Prince Maharaj Kumar Hanwant Singh was going to get married to the Princess of Dhrangdhara, in Saurashtra, and the whole town would attend. It sounded pretty interesting but all Brits still had to be careful where they went, especially military and especially military in crowds, so I asked Les what he thought of it.

'Well it beats hunting scorpions or watching polo. Should be a good 'crack', let's do it.' Then he paused a moment. 'Tell you what. I'll have a word with Josh, over by the hangar.'

'Who's Josh then?'

'He's one of Singe's lot, on the servicing crew. When we came here, we gave them a 'hand' to move some of their equipment, to give us some hangar space.'

'Oh, right.' My frown showed I was a little doubtful.

'Yeah, he's OK. More airframes really and servicing. I helped them out with some hydraulics to get things moving.'

This sounded quite good. Local knowledge and local contacts. The upshot of it was that Josh wasn't going to miss it at all. Les and myself agreed to meet him and go into town on the 14th to have a look.

Jodhpur Town Plan - 1933

Legend

1	Clock Tower and Sardar Market
2	Sojita Gate
3	Umed Hospital
4	Wyndham Hospital
5	Railway Station next to Post Office
6	Power House
7	Jail
8	Police Unit
9	Jaswant College
10	D. H. School
11	Willingdon Gardens
12	1st Lawn Polo Ground
13	2nd. Lawn Polo Ground
14	Golf Course
15	Sardar Club
16	Polo Club
17	Hotel

5. Jodhpur Town Plan, 1933

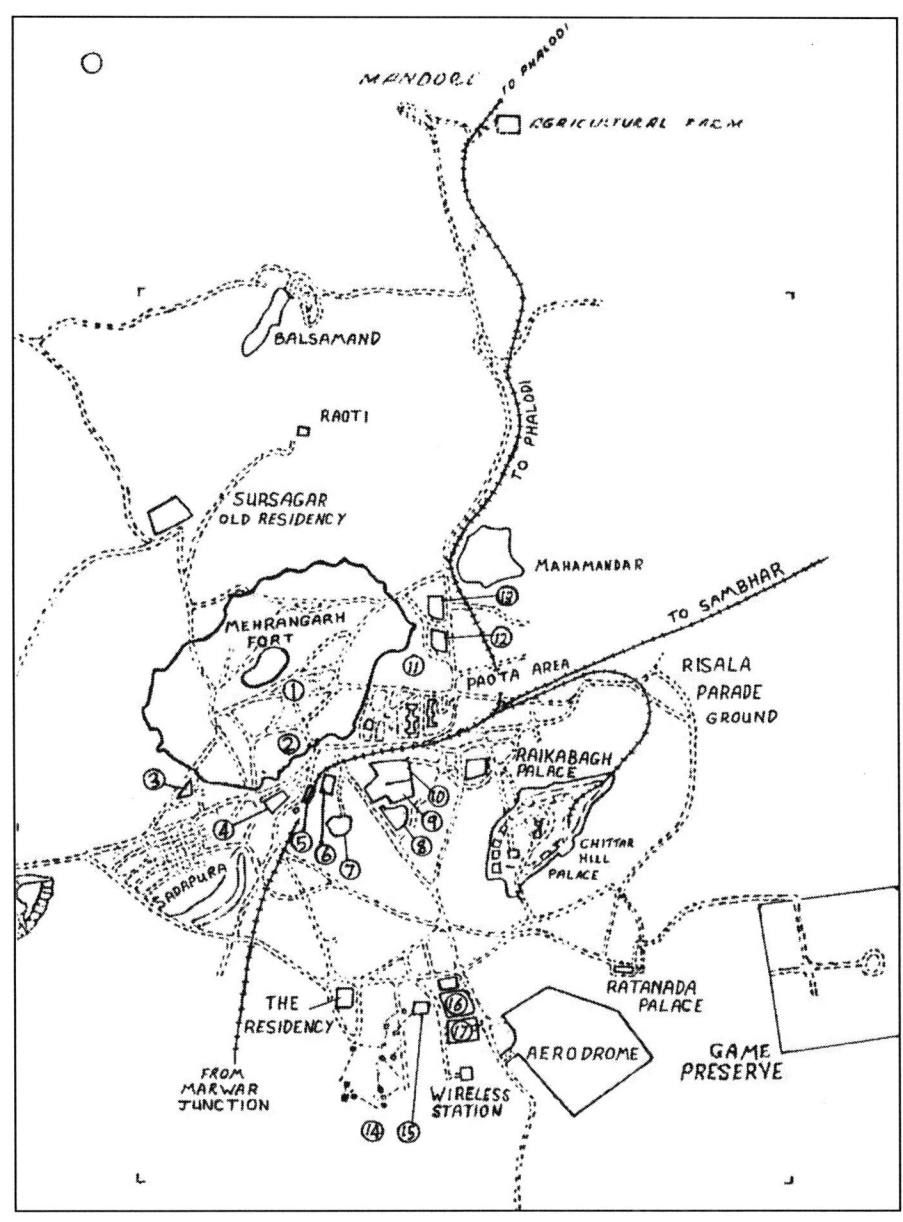

Supplied by kind permission of H. H. Maharaja Umaid Singhji.

CHAPTER TWELVE
The Wedding

We'd arranged to meet Josh by the main entrance to the camp around 11 am when we'd make our way into town about a mile and a half away. Without batting an eyelid Les introduced me to Josh as Commando Kenny. This had the predicted instant effect of causing me embarrassment, as good mates do, and making Josh feel awkward as he didn't know what to make of it. We set off for the town in the hot sun and by the time I had explained about it we knew each other! He seemed a sociable chap with good enough English. While we were still on the outskirts I saw a small field with the clay bells in and asked Josh about them. I had to explain what a 'bell' was in English first but when I had explained he burst into laughter. He was surprised none of us knew and went on to explain all the 'cow pats' that the holy cattle leave behind are gathered up when semi dry and placed on edge in small fields to completely dry in circular layers gradually tapering as they get higher. My clay bells were well placed piles of shit! But it was shit that burnt well and was used as fuel by the locals.

As we neared the town it seemed unusually quiet almost deserted. That is until we got right to the centre when apart from the noise, it became obvious why as it must be every person in Jodhpur had turned up to jostle and squeeze in to the town centre and as resourceful as the Indians are, on to any balcony ledge or roof that would give a view of the forthcoming procession. The clock tower which is a very impressive Victorian stone tower about one hundred feet tall with balconies at different levels was full of people in multi-coloured clothing, some of them just clinging to the outside.

It was customary that our first 'port of call' was to Premvillas and it was a relief to escape the hubbub of the crowds as we entered the bar. After a couple of beers (juice for Josh) and a chipatti each we concluded that we were well placed to accept the arrival of the Maharaja and his new wife. Josh took advantage of the interlude to tell us a little about the royal 'house' we were waiting for.

Evidently it was to be the wedding of the Maharaja of Jodhpur's son Prince Maharaj Kumer Hanwant Singh to the Princess of Dhrangdhara, in Saurashtra in the west of the country. They would get married in one of the temples within the Mehrangarh Fort. Then there would be a large procession through city. As we were here for the procession that was going to be on such a grand scale, from the point of view of a chap that had been married just seven months it did beg a question of comparison. I was inwardly shamed a little as I couldn't tell Josh anywhere near as much about British weddings as he could about the Hindu ones but he told us that no matter what level people were in Hindu society the basic stages were the same but some had more stages than others. As Josh now had a captive audience my enquiry was to be answered in full.

He explained that the Pujari is a Hindu temple priest responsible for performing the temple rituals and prayer services and they acted as councillors during Hindu festivities and festivals. The Dowry for the Marharini (bride) would be gold and silver utensils and for example in the case of wealthy Marharajas, cases of expensive shawls and ornaments, jewels and silk material and brocade dresses. I could easily see how this related to 'our' idea of wedding presents. He continued to explain how there are lots of stages to a wedding and one of them is when tokens of love are exchanged. That did make me wonder about British weddings and rings being exchanged. The key stage though is when the Pujari creates a sacred fire, a Pious fire, when the bride and groom join shawls by knotting them then perform the Saat Pheres or Seven Rounds while others perform sanskript readings to holy chants expressing felicitations for the Maharaja. When we quizzed him about a 'round' Josh explained that the joined couple walked around the Pious Fire for each one of the couples holy blessings which he proceeded to tell us. First was to earn and provide a living for their household or family and to avoid those things that might harm them. Second was to build their physical, mental and spiritual powers and to lead to a healthy lifestyle. Third was to earn and increase their wealth by righteous and proper means. The fourth was to acquire knowledge, happiness and harmony by mutual love, respect, understanding and faith. Number five was to have children for whom they will be responsible and blessed with healthy, righteous and brave children. Number six was to have self control and longevity and finally the seventh was to be true to each other, loyal and remain lifelong companions joined in holy wedlock. We were both impressed by the in depth knowledge Josh held but the whole thing seemed far more comprehensive than the British love honour and obey 'thing' but I suppose a promise is a promise anywhere.

The whole service is followed by a very elaborate reception with feasting and events take place over two or three days like lancing demonstrations and swordsmanship followed by traditional dancing and performances by local entertainers like snake charmers, fire eaters and displays of camels and elephants. That part did seem a bit over and above the British wedding reception but clearly there was a comparison. I didn't know what Josh felt like after all that but just thinking about what he said made us both thirsty. It wasn't too long before there was an increase in the commotion outside and looking through the window it seemed everyone was trying to 'escape' to the right. Josh was most eager that we should stand on our chairs by the window as the procession was due to approach which compared to the hoards of people milling around outside in the dust and the sun seemed a pretty good option.

A few moments later the crowd started re-emerging from the right making way for the imminent entourage. A squad of the Jodhpur Rasala (cavalry) first appeared and apparently established a clear passage for the representations of the Maharajas 'Royal' House. The Infantry came next which seemed a very clear demonstration of authority yet next, in total contrast was the first contingent of dancing girls and they were a sight for sore eyes. A host of young lithsome bodies, well decorated and wearing thin flowing materials in lavish colours of pinks, reds, greens and mauve that moved in unison to the strange sounding music emanating from something that looked like a band with some even stranger looking musical instruments. I could see Josh was really proud to be witnessing the event and he told us the material the girls wore was very expensive and the colours were expensive to produce, so this was a further demonstration of wealth and position. By now there was a throng of chants and blessings being shouted by the people and it was really noisy. But that was nothing to what came next as behind the 'music' came the first of a string of magnificent elephants. The leading one carried a Royal Officer who had a large pannier basket on either side of him. It was difficult to see at first just what he was doing but whatever it was, it prompted everyone around him to bow to the ground. I was amazed at the respect and subservience this presence instilled en mass but maybe it wasn't too surprising as right behind was the most magnificent spectacle. It must have been the largest elephant in India that followed but it was so bedecked with lavish covers full of colour and gold decorations there was little of it to be seen but ones eye was automatically drawn to the Howdah it carried which transported the Maharaja and his Maharani. Every part of sparkled from the gold finials at each corner, along the sides with jewels and gold and silver decoration to the strappings of fantastic colours. The couple were both immaculately presented and were seated as they were gently swayed side to side by the motion of the beast of beasts. You couldn't help but be impressed and I reckoned the poor locals must be in absolute awe of the whole event. There followed nearly a dozen more elephants all highly decorated and presumably representing various elements of the royal household. That clearly was the highlight but it seems the Maharaja would have the full extent of his wealth demonstrated as a herd of Arabian Ponies were paraded next with Buffalo and Oxen behind. The rear was taken up by the Camel Corps in all their finery. It had gone a little quieter now so I asked Josh about the lead elephant and the effect it had. He was pleased to know of my interest and explained that it was a big demonstration of how generous the His Royal Highness is towards his people. Josh could see that I was a little confused by his answer. So my next question wasn't surprising.

'So how is making people bow down in front of him generous?' I asked.

Now it was Josh that looked confused. He paused, maybe trying to understand my 'English' way of thinking. Then his face brightened.

'The leading Officer' he said, 'with the large baskets either side?'

'Yes.' I said.

'Those baskets are full of gold and silver Mohurs (Indian coins). The leading Officer is giving the people all the money!'

'You're serious aren't you?' This was hard to believe.

'Oh yes,' he continued 'each basket will hold a Lakh.' I was dumb struck but then asked what a Lakh was.

'But that is 100,000 silver rupees,' he said, smiling.

'Les! Have you heard this?' I indicated to Josh. Les shook his head.

'Josh, do us a favour will you and tell Les what you told me.' He smiled at another opportunity.

As the last of the Royal Forces passed by the crowds closed in behind and began a steady drift following the courtage we stepped down from the window. Whatever purpose it served, the whole event of the procession with the people and the atmosphere let alone the extravagance was unforgettable. None of us had a lot to say because Josh was beaming with pride and we were quite lost for words as we had never experienced anything like the grandeur we had just witnessed. We agreed that it seemed most civil to share in the celebrations by having another drink.

About two days later I started feeling really sick. I had head aches, sweating and shivers. I reported sick and was told straight away I had Malaria. I was prescribed the standard treatment for Malaria which was an eighteen day course starting with five days on liquid Quinine then five days on Mapacin tablets, followed by two days abstinence then five days of Pamaquin tablets.

A good alternative to visiting the town was the Deoli House which was a club for RAF personnel and was situated a couple of miles south of the town and a mile or so away from camp with only sparse trees and shrub land in between. It was a modest size and was run by women from the WRVS. They served really nice tea and non-alcoholic drinks there and sandwiches and cakes etc. It was a nice place to relax, have a chat or write letters, just very comfortable and in the evenings it was quite a pleasant walk. It was only a couple of weeks after my first bout of Malaria that I got really sick again but this time with dysentery which gave you stomach cramps and diarrhoea. It was of little consolation to be told that nearly everyone got it sooner or later out here.

Not all our trips out involved 'Premvillas' as once we got to know Josh a bit sometimes he would come with Ian and me for a trip into the town. It was quite refreshing to know what we were looking at in the bazaars and not to be over charged and he often took us to see just some of the amazing temples that seemed to be all over the place. The extent of the statues and symbolism of so much mystical heritage was difficult to comprehend but we just accepted that it was everywhere. We saw the wall of hands in Loha Pul (The Iron Gate) which is one of about a dozen vast gate house buildings along the tremendous outer wall that encapsulates the Mehrangarh Fort originally protecting the old town and leading to a temple of the Goddess 'Chamunda' who is the Goddess of Shakti power. As Josh was with us we could experience the full diversity of the bazaars and different produce and what to try and what not to try! Josh pointed out the Bhajis. There were all types but they all looked similar, the difference was the Chile ones 'blew your head off' while the potato ones were very nice. Along the way were stalls selling Kotis which were like round flat bread held a bit like a bowl with a savoury filling in the middle. One of the drinks that tasted OK was a Laasi. It was a creamy milk drink that was sweet and usually cold. In the streets there was every kind of stall including 'grog shops' where you were offered samples to make a selection. In the town there was one moochi walla, a cobbler who was very worthwhile. In half an hour he could produce a very decent pair of shoes for 8 rupees, while you waited, or had a couple of drinks.

Mac that I'd met on the boat was still a typical miserable Scots but he was in charge of us at the Armoury and he wasn't too bad. He often tagged along with Ian and myself and we had many interesting visits to the city and sometimes with a few other lads.

Occasionally wild dogs used to venture into the town at night scavenging for food and quite often used to howl somewhat. One night Danny and I were walking back to camp from Deolis in the evening and as we got back to camp one dog in particular was howling and we were both pretty fed up with it. We located the dog at some distance by an oil drum or something next to a building under construction. I reckoned that the nuisance justified an exercise in night vision and target practice. I couldn't see it clearly but I released the old Berretta and let rip at the dog and the drum. One of them yelped and the dog shot off in to the night and stopped howling! On another occasion, I was only going to the NAAFI from our billet and came across a Silver Krait which is a small snake, about a foot long, ¾ in dia. but deadly poisonous. I wasn't going to create a disturbance by having a shot at it in the middle of the domestic site but it was a reminder that you always had to be careful.

Around March and April the weather really started warming up which reduced the amount of Malaria outbreaks. I had just had my second and in May and June it could easily be a 120°F in the shade so our stone barrack room was bestowed with a 'punkah' which looked like a large carpet supported at the top of the roof with a thin rope connected lower down which went to the outside. There was local lad (punkah walla) stationed outside, sat against the wall of our barrack room with the same piece of rope looped over the end of his big toe. By moving his leg up and down he swung the 'punkah' which gave some sort of air circulation. Sometimes he would nod off to sleep and the 'fan' would stop, then we would swing on the rope and the boy would be hoisted up by his big toe, which woke him up!

A rather unexpected turn of events occurred at the end of April in the form of a summons to our Flight Sergeant. It really was unexpected as I was certain I hadn't 'stepped out of line' for some weeks now and I couldn't imagine any justification for it, but just sometimes it goes to show just how priceless the unexpected can be. It was certainly a good indication that I wasn't being escorted over there. After being told to 'stand easy', almost without any preamble the Flight Sergeant told me that it was his pleasure to award me the promotion to the rank of Corporal with effect from the 1 May. He added

'in all theatres of war conditions were rarely good but especially now, in the face of the Japanese advance, the service and Great Britain was dependant on every man doing his job to the best of his ability.'

'Yes, Flight.'

'Dismiss.'

That was a 'turn up for the books' and gave me a few more things to think about. I think it would be a good time to have a chat with Charlie.

CHAPTER THIRTEEN
Beaufort Inspection

I was familiar with most of the duties of Corporals but one of the key roles was attending the pilots debrief after their missions to take notes of armourment faults or requirements. Another one of the key duties on a 'front line' airfield was Harmonizing the guns to the Sights. This made sure that the aircraft guns were pointing or harmonized to the aiming sight that the pilot used. No matter how good the pilots were, unless the guns hit the target that the pilot was aiming at we'd lose the war very quickly. If the guns had been changed or adjusted they would probably need resetting and round here especially we all wanted them to be good. In the process of their inspection the riggers would have the aircraft jacked up on trestles. The ring and bead sight in the cockpit was aligned to a 400 yd marker (a disc on a post); the guns were then set to target the marker giving a spray pattern before or after that point. Some pilots occasionally requested the guns set at a closer distance, down to 250 yds, but this was unofficial. The breach block of each cannon was cocked. A special periscope tool was fitted to the breach block of each cannon in turn. By looking through the barrel via the periscope, each cannon was adjusted by jack screws to align on the marker with a similar adjustment for lateral movement. When 'camera guns' were fitted they were looked after by the Photographic crew so that when the guns were fired the camera was operated pneumatically by a connecting copper pipe.

I didn't smoke cigarettes as such; I used to give my Woodbine ration of 50 cigs. per man per week, to Clancy our bearer. Instead I used to get Burma Cheroot Cigars, about 7 in. long and not too fat. They came in boxes of 100 costing about 6s 6d. They had a lovely strong aroma that usually overcame some of the more local pungent ones especially when we were in town but the ladies at the Deoli Club weren't very impressed! I really enjoyed one in the evening when it became cooler.

On one particular week, I had been working on the gun turret hydraulics of a Beaufort torpedo Bomber, having to check the pump operation, rebuild the control valve and then bleed the system.

6. A Bristol Beaufort similar to the ill-fated Beaufort DW941. Copyright of AirTeamImages.com.

A couple of engine fitters were doing some routine maintenance on the 14 cylinder radial Pegasus engines. The pilot and wireless op/gunner were hanging around, doing a few checks on the plane and having a chat with us. They were friendly and helpful and told me they were good friends as they had been in training together in Canada. A crew of four normally operated the Beaufort and usually they were moved as a crew with Ullerthorne being the navigator but they had told me they were a gunner short. They knew the work I had been doing and they also knew that to test the system and the operation of the turret the port engine had to be running to supply the power. Even in more temperate climates the radial engines easily overheated so out in the desert in 100° plus heat there was no chance of a ground test whatsoever. A test flight was arranged for the following day 4 May at 0930 hrs, before it got too warm and I was to be a substitute rear gunner to check the turret. I was looking forward to it as this would be my first 'twin engine' flight in Jodhpur. That evening I told Danny about it in our billet as I explained.

'What? To test the turret and hydraulics?' he queried.

'Yeah, and the engines have been serviced as well.' I added, trying to establish the importance of the event.

'Well it looks like you can rely on it being good weather, at any rate.' He paused briefly. 'Do you remember what you told me about those Fortress 1's, the 17c? About how they iced up and tended to catch fire?' Danny's darker side was a pragmatist.

'Yeah, I know, but they were brand new aircraft. They had a few problems to sort out.'

'That's true, but they were expensive problems. That's all.' There was no denying it.

'Anyway,' I countered 'the Beaufort's have been out a few years now. Loads of squadrons have them.'

'Yeah,' he said sharply 'and most of them are Australian or Canadian.' I wasn't sure of the relevance, but it was true that the pilot and his wireless operator were Canadian. I shrugged at his comment.

'All I'll say,' He continued, 'is that an engine fitter mate of mine told me that the Beaufort's are pretty good while they have two engines running. If one packs up, you're in trouble.'

'Yeah, OK'. I still wanted to look forward to my flight so I didn't pursue it. But, I wouldn't ignore what Danny said either.

The following day I got kitted out for the flight nice and early and got a lift over to dispersal where I met the others at the plane. There were a couple of engine fitters with a starting trolley and as I approached I heard one of them mention about a low magneto (ignition) drop of 200 to the pilot but he shrugged it off and made some comment about the dry atmosphere. I was pretty sure that a magneto drop of no more than 150 was acceptable. I didn't say anything but I was well aware that just like on the old Matchless, the magneto was imperative for the engines to run. The pilot talked us through the intended flight details of take off, height, direction and duration then we clambered into the plane to our respective positions and after a few moments the port engine fired up followed closely by the starboard engine. I think everyone had a lot of respect for the flying crew as it was their lives on the 'line' so to speak but when it came to knowing about the engines and airframes, the ground crew were up there with the front runners. Both engines had started smart enough and ran quite evenly at low revs but when the revs were increased to begin taxiing the starboard side had a slight miss-fire. This was quite common with cold engines and usually 'cleared' when the engines warmed up on taxiing. There was absolutely no reason to have any doubts about anything. It was a beautiful day, as it usually was and all the routine checks had not high lighted anything of consequence, apart from a low magneto reading. As we taxied I had my head and shoulders out of the hatch port side listening to the engine but I thought 'the driver knows best' and left it at that, well nearly. As the gun turret is a 'mid upper' it is located about half way along the top of the aircraft with my 'exit' hatch just in front on the port side. All of us entered by a hatch on the underside of the fuselage at the front. There are other hatches on the sides, but they are all at the front with the exception of the mid escape hatch, specifically for the mid-gunner. I was well aware of this, as I was also well aware that 'my' hatch required two distinct movements to open it. The first was to release the full anchor system that totally secured it and the second was a simple latch for convenience of operation. I thought it would be a good idea to keep the first stage released until both engines were warmed up. We travelled along the peritrack to the end of the runway where the pilot would make a final check of the instruments and controls before take off. I went forward through the mid bulkhead to tell the pilot to select 'Turret' on the hydraulics lever. He reached for a switch and gave me the thumbs up without looking round. As I was returning along the fuselage I released the first stage fastening of the hatch with a little thought for Danny as the engines increased revs for take off and I took up my position of mid-gunner and strapped myself in.

The engines were steadied at mid revs, most likely for the oil pressure to be established then were increased to about 80% at 1,800 to 1,900 rpm which without any bomb load would be more than adequate. The flaps were down and the air brakes released. As the whole fuselage resonated with the throbbing vibration of twenty-eight cylinders and 51 litres of engine powering up we lurched forward to build up speed. I remember thinking only a few years back how I was impressed with the power and speed of my 350 cc Raleigh motorcycle (before the Matchless). What I was in now was so far beyond the 350 it wasn't funny, and impressed? You'd have to be dead not to be! We built up speed sharpish enough and I was impressed as to how good the condition was of Mr. Singhe's runway, not too many bumps. We were really motoring now as the tail lifted us to the horizontal and I could feel the weight coming off the suspension and on to the airframe. There were a couple of light skips of the wheels then the pilot pulled the stick back and we were climbing at about thirty degrees up into the sky blue yonder. After a few seconds the undercarriage started to retract and I was getting a brilliant view of the airfield and feeling quite pleased with myself. We must have been at about 400 ft when we clearly started banking to the left, as was expected. While we had been taking off and climbing in a straight line gravity had been acting on everything vertically downwards but as soon as we started banking the aircraft took on a steeper plane as the starboard aerolons gave more lift and pulled us upwards through a large arc. Then as if from nowhere it was like a thunderbolt struck the starboard engine but there was no thunder or lightning for 600 miles. As quick as I could realize what had happened I heard the Port engine revs increase and become strained as the pilot instantly gave full power to the engine and feathered the propeller for maximum thrust. I felt the twitch of the fuselage as opposite rudder was applied to increase the lift. I went to the small portal where I could see a black stream of oil vapour and smoke trailing behind us and realized there was no way it was going to restart let alone run. I'd got a sudden really sick feeling in my stomach. Stupidly I desperately started thinking of what our options might be but quickly realized that it didn't matter two hoots what I thought, the pilot was at the controls and at 400 ft, not even parachutes were any use. We didn't have enough power for level flight and we didn't have enough height to pick up speed. Our starboard wing was still low and I knew that if it didn't come up, then we were going down. The seconds ticked by as the fuselage vibrated from the strain of maximum power from the port engine. We were losing height steadily now and the wing hadn't come up and at less than 400 ft now, there isn't much time to try anything. I had stopped feeling sick by now as really I was feeling shit scared. I thought about the Hampden crash and the fire and knew there was probably about 150 gallons of high octane fuel on either side of me. I wanted to either get out or be killed on impact. I dreaded the thought of being on fire. We were going to crash in a few seconds and couldn't do anything about it. Well the truth is I couldn't do much about it. I knew that I had partially released the escape hatch but realized I would have to be able to get out of it to survive. In any impact you are thrown forwards so I unstrapped myself and took position against the bulkhead across the fuselage as it was the only barrier to a straight trajectory up to the cockpit. It was less than two feet wide and a bit of a gamble, but it was my only hope. I pushed my back into it as hard as I could with my legs with my right arm along the fuselage and my left arm braced across at the top and waited and seriously wondered whether I would be killed outright or be burnt to death. Is it going to be ten seconds or will it be five? Is there any point in counting or will it... There was a monumentous grawnshing noise momentarily as the tip of the starboard wing ground into the desert then swung the whole plane down nose first into the ground. The lightweight aluminium nose shell just crumpled up as six tons of a plane impacted at about 130 mph and violently slammed me against the bulkhead in the process. The momentum carried us along for about another 150 yards while the nose and front fuselage were crushed into the ground. Half way along, the starboard engine was ripped off with the wing and allowed the contents of the fuel tanks to freely disperse.

The port propeller had been all folded back on itself now and with all the ripped fuel lines and the red hot exhaust duct the fuel was ignited as we came to a stop. God knows how, but I was conscious and I was still in the fuselage. I was stunned and felt like I'd just been hit by a train from behind but I had to 'get with it', my life depended on it. The far side of the fuselage was already getting hot as I smelled burning material. I tried to move but my left arm felt like it was stuck. I tried again then realized it wasn't stuck, it just wouldn't move and hurt like hell. I'd broken something and still had to get out. I could hear shouting and screaming from up the front which had flames inside as the fuselage started filling with fumes and smoke. It encouraged me as I got myself turned and strained my right arm out to the handle of the escape hatch. Once hold of it I only had one slight turn to open it but my hand was wet from wiping the blood from my face. By now burning paint and oil fumes were filling the fuselage and the panels were buckling from the heat on the other side. With total determination I opened the hatch and desperately climbed down on to the wing and then the ground and ran as best I could, just enough to get some distance from the plane. I stopped and turned and wiped the blood from my face and looked around. I was dumbfounded and realized that 'plane' was a bit of an overstatement. There was no plane to be recognized as there was only the semi-skeleton of the fuselage that was a mass of dirty yellow flame being immediately transformed into thick black acrid smoke that billowed skywards. Even the ground around the plane was on fire from the spilt fuel and there was Ullerthorne, staggering around and blackened with his arm right across his eyes and blood over his face. He couldn't see a thing and was wandering back towards the flaming wreck. I didn't have to think twice because the lad had no chance at all. I ran and got to him as quickly as I could. He was shouting for just anybody. I just grabbed his other arm and led him to safety. It looked like he'd got a face full of instrument panel but he was safe. I turned to view the wreck as best I could as there were still two more of us somewhere. I knew there was no hope for one of them as I could hear the stomach churning screams of the navigator, trapped and burning in the aircraft, until fumes and smoke made him oblivious of his fate. I wiped my face again to have another look and was amazed to see the fourth person close to where the nose would have been. He was close to the flames with his trousers ripped and bloodied. I went over to him. It was the pilot. He was just stood there, shaking and staring at the flames. His face was all singed, his hands were burned and his jacket was still smoking. He was just muttering over and over through his tears 'I just couldn't get him. I just couldn't get him', with only a silent warm south easterly to dry his tears. All we could do was watch this inferno of devastation as the navigator was in his own funeral pyre.

The distant noise of the approaching fire tender instilled us to mumbled comments of consolation. As the tender approached, some parts of the aircraft were now melting and really nothing could be done to any effect, so it wasn't too frustrating to find that the only asbestos fire suit on board wouldn't fit anyone. The heat was now so intense that no one in any suit could have got near it. Soon afterwards an ambulance arrived and took Ullerthorne on a stretcher while the pilot and myself sat in the back. We were taken to Windham Hospital on the west side of the town. It seemed that I had got spinal injuries from having it massaged by the Beaufort, a broken shoulder and a fair gash across my right eye and cheek, with cuts and bruises. The pilot was lucky as he had burned his hands and got a nasty cut on his leg but Ullerthorne was taken to Karachi hospital where his hand was amputated. I had eight weeks in Windham Hospital, located on the west side of the town. For the first two weeks any movement was near agony but week by week as the pain reduced my movement increased. The circumstances forced me back to the time when I was last in bed for so long and quite ill. I was nine years old and developed what I was told to be Rheumatic Fever. I felt terrible then as well by constantly feeling sick and aching all over with my joints really hurting. I must have been off school for nearly six months which is probably why old Llewy seemed so clever. It wasn't a pleasant time then as it wasn't now and just like then I could hardly do anything as well. I was really bored and frustrated but it did give me the opportunity to write a nice letter to Elsie. I wrote it in the hope that it might arrive for her birthday on 29 May but god only knows when she might receive it. It was nice that Ian, Mac and Danny visited sometimes and maintained my stock of cigars. During my stay a fitter IIE was admitted with both hands heavily bandaged but it was a while before I realized one was shorter than the other. He had been swinging the propeller of a Tigermoth biplane to start it but it backfired and sheared off his right hand and severely cut his left. Overall, I was so relieved that I was recovering as there were people in there with some terrible problems. After five or six weeks I was allowed out in the town for short periods as part of my recovery.

After eight weeks I was still feeling a bit stiff but otherwise not too bad and got booked in to see the MO again. Danny picked me up from the hospital in a truck to take me to see him on the domestic site. Before we got there though, we took a detour to see the crash site. It was a great black area decorated with glistening pools of shiny aluminium. The only clue of an aircraft was the steel chassis of the gun mounts and a couple of mounds left from the wheels with black snake like pieces of half burnt hydraulic hose dotted around. The engines had been removed to a hanger for inspection and I didn't want to look too closely where young Measor met his fate but I hoped his remains had been dealt with. Viewing such blatant and total destruction gave me a slightly nauseous feeling as I thought of him. Silently I paid my respects. A distant voice in the back of my brain kept telling me 'There but for the grace of God, go I'.

'Come on Kenny. You don't want to be dwelling on that too much. Let's get you over to the MO'.

I just got back in the truck.

The MO checked me over and seemed quite satisfied with my progress but thought that I wasn't really fit enough yet. 'It might be a good idea to have a couple of week's recuperation at Simla'

I agreed with him straight away. I'd never heard of Simla. I had no idea where it was and no idea how to get there but I couldn't have agreed more! He said there was a Lockheed Hudson leaving for Delhi shortly as he wrote out the authorisation. 'Make sure you're on it!' he said as he handed me the 'chit'. I assured him that I would be.

CHAPTER FOURTEEN
We go Paddling

When I found Charlie, he was really pleased to see me and he said he would pass on what the MO had said and wished me well. Danny took me out to dispersal and I boarded a Lockheed Hudson bound for Delhi. We were to have two Hurricanes as an escort. We got airborne OK and set on course. After a short while we realised that we had lost the Hurricanes, they had returned to Jodhpur as their radios had gone u/s. I didn't think that was too bad as we were heading west, well away from any trouble but the bottom fell out of my little world when I was told that as we no longer had an escort, we had to return to base also. I was pretty annoyed about the situation but I was determined not to be done out of my two weeks at Simla so as soon as we landed I went to the Railway Transport Office and got a rail pass. It was only then that I realized just where it was, more or less due north of us and set right in the slopes of the Himalayas.

Late in the afternoon I got the night train to Delhi. The compartment I got in was second class but was only occupied by a soldier. We exchanged greetings and I made myself comfortable. Shortly before the train was due to pull out some local chap entered and started filling the compartment up with 'hell and all' things. We soon kicked him out making it quite clear that we were suggesting the third class carriages! 'chali ojow'. We bumped and rattled our way to Delhi through the night and arrived quite early, found some breakfast then resigned ourselves to a little sightseeing there. We took a rickshaw ride round the city and had lunch there. Afterwards we made our way to Old Delhi and had a look round the impressive Red Fort there. It's a very large ornate building with two highly positioned domes at either side with peculiar decoration across the front at the very top and commanded a very dominant outlook across the town. There was an open type of court area immediately in front and a little further out at the front a road travelled across with trees here and there, along it.

Later in the afternoon we parted company then I made my way back to the station and found the North Line to catch the Delhi - Ambala - Kalka train on the narrow gauge railway. The carriages were smaller but still fairly comfortable and really no noisier than the other trains. It was a pleasant journey but as the hills increased so did the twisting of the track so much so that several times I saw the rear of the train while sitting in the forward part.

All the time though, we were steadily climbing. In Kalka we then changed to the peculiar looking rack and pinion train bound for Simla. We started off OK but very quickly the gradients increased quite alarmingly to the point that if they had been roads I would have questioned whether I would have driven up them. I just hoped the engineers who installed the rack and pinion were good at their job. At 9,000 ft we finally reached Simla which apart from being individual in its characteristics and location was a place that one had to get accustomed to because of the rarefied atmosphere at this altitude. From the railway station I took a rickshaw to the YMCA hostel where I was to stay. It was located just off the main street which was a very steep hill, a little way up another hill. In general the whole of the town was sitting on the side of a small mountain and it became clear to see why the Tibetan porters were such a rare breed. They all had a turban type head dress which accepted a strong band which went backwards to support whatever vast loads were on their backs and every one of them had very broad shoulders and powerful stocky legs. My accommodation was quite reasonable and with no itinerary to hand the next two weeks showed promise to be most pleasant in such a pretty town and a magnificent area being only 182 miles from Tibet. It seems that until 1819 Simla was just another hill village of the Nepalese kingdom but during the Victorian era the toffs of the civil and military empire builders found the green pastures just below and the snow capped peaks just above were blessed with a cool and remarkably fresh atmosphere. Hence in 1864 Simla was declared as the summer capital of India and became a 'hill station'. As a result of this, Christ Church with its red tile roof and square tower on The Ridge and the main street of shops that lay 'east to west' in the town a little lower all looked most typically Victorian as were so many other buildings.

All types of people were posted to hill stations, mostly for leave or recuperation and at Simla the cafes, shops, bazaar and local places to explore, lended itself to it ideally. One of the most impressive places nearby was the grand Vice Regal Lodge which with its six floors and elaborate architecture could quite appropriately have been called a palace. In reality it was the Viscounts Royal Summer Residence. A little above the town was the small village of Jakhu which stood at the top of Jakhu Hill and was crowned by a temple to the Lord Hanuman. I was there only long enough to find the monkeys, that were so prolific, only interesting rather than a nuisance. After two weeks of exploring the area and eating reasonably well, I had to use my return ticket to Jodhpur.

I arrived on camp at Jodhpur but still maintained to be sick for a couple of days. After a few discreet enquiries I found the official cause of the accident was put down to 'Hydraulicing' which happens when amounts of oil get into the engine cylinders which cannot compress it, so blows the engine apart. It was a bit peculiar though as after a radial engined aircraft had been stood for any amount of time, the engine had to be turned backwards to allow any oil in the lower cylinders to drain out. Also, both engines were running on take-off!

Just over a week after my return from Simla, Les Morley told me he had managed a ride in a Beaufort. I sarcastically enquired as to whether it actually 'took off' and added that I thought he was sticking his neck out a bit after my crash. He said that it had crossed his mind, but he was so bored doing sod all, it just seemed a good idea. He said that he did find it a bit un-nerving when it needed three attempts at take-off though. One engine kept cutting out at full RPM, but after an engine fitter tweaked the mixture screw he said they took off OK and it was great.

Barely two weeks had passed since my return to camp in mid-July and I was over at dispersal with Danny and Les on servicing work getting back into the routine of things. It had only been a couple of days before when I was in Premvillas catching up on events that I heard there was some local concern because a few of the local wells had died up because the monsoons were late and this had dire consequences for every family affected. Yet for the last ten days or so there had been heavy cloud overhead on many occasions but it had never 'broke' into rain, it just held up there, thick grey cloud gently floating by but the river that ran round the edge of the camp told a different story. It seemed a bit peculiar working out at dispersal in shirt and shorts with a humid warm breeze blowing but with heavy overcast skies, yet for the last week or so the water level had been slowly rising which was almost insignificant but the water flowing by had come from the Himalayas about 300 miles north where the monsoons had already broken. That in itself did not affect the RAF one jot, until the monsoon broke over Jodhpur. We were just about to break for lunch when all of us felt the first drops of the monsoon rains. As the first drops fell on the concrete they left a wet area larger than a half crown but within two minutes it fell as a total deluge and it fell everywhere. Les had seen the monsoon rains before and even though we hadn't, we didn't need telling. What we really needed was to get out of the place which was easier said than done as the nearest cover was over a mile away. Straight away the downpour was drumming on the aircraft wings and within two minutes all of us were soaked through so whatever we might have chosen to do became incidental. All we could do was make the aircraft safe with all the panels back on and return to the domestic site. The three of us set of across the airfield completely soaked with the rain pouring down everywhere just like the proverbial 'stair rods'. All of us had great clods of muddy sand where our boots should have been with the rain pouring off every extremity as we plodded our way back. After we had all been cursing about the weather and being soaked and the mud, another aspect was slowly being realised. For six months now the entire airfield had been hot sandy scrub land and nobody ever gave a thought to the tracks that the service trucks used. But we were thinking about them now because they had been transformed from tracks into rivers and a good few were between us and the domestic site. As we had to cross them no one knew if the water was six inches or three feet deep and some were flowing at a fair rate of knots which had made a walk back to camp something of a serious event. We realised we had to be careful and each of us anchored ourselves for the others as we got in and out of the rivers but even when we were three hundred yards from the site it was obvious there was no rush as over half the tented site was flooded and it was still raining just as hard. The lovely pristine Control Tower now seemed more suited to being a Lighthouse. By now there was only the occasional rise of land, like islands in a lake, that was above water and although we were tempted to make for them we had underestimated just how much wildlife this 'barren' scrub land held. All the snakes, spiders, scorpions as well as the beetles were all making for any dry land and being on any of the rises one encountered the entire cross section of wild life that the desert had to offer including a couple of porcupines. As soon as we realised, we stayed in the water. When we actually reached the domestic site there were men shouting orders and others carrying whatever was deemed to be important at the time. A number of the tents were now being washed away as the tent pegs had no hold in the water thus exposing bedding and uniforms and anything within them to the continued deluge. We found a couple of the armourers then Charlie. He told us the same as the others, which was to get any setting tools, guns and ammunition to higher ground, like on to the back of the trucks for example. So we 'set to' just scouting round for equipment in the water or moving the boxes as we could see them. By this time there wasn't a single tent left in tact, anything that floated had gone somewhere and anything else was under water which was mostly above the wheels of the trucks. The domestic site had gone, there were only a couple of stone billets and the mess intact albeit flooded. There was no option but for the fifty or so of us in the middle of it all to head for the control tower and service area. A further situation now presented itself as at the start of it all the three of us had waded across the flooded tracks to get to the others but for all of us to get to the service area and safety, a deeper section had to be crossed. It was wide and flowing. There was some discussion and as we had no equipment it was decided for all of us to link arms in a line and attempt to get across. It was quite hairy as there were now acres of water all around and no one knew just how deep the crossing would be. Step by step the front man led the human caterpillar towards the crossing. We could tell the main route of it from the waters surface and when the front man suddenly went in up his waist he knew he was there but progressed carefully but even so he missed his footing and sunk to his chest. Continuing on it was obvious he was struggling against the flow and now the third man was up to his waist. By the time the seventh man was getting deeper the lead man was rising up then the water was below his hips. We had got the human bridge. Slowly each one of us in turn entered the water and waded across. It was reminiscent of some weird chorus line in a theatre with a load of men soaked in shirts and shorts and clodded boots shuffling with linked arms into the water. What had been our camp in the desert half an hour ago was now a huge lake with pieces of furniture, peoples belongings, rubbish and just everything now floating all over the site. All of us made it to the hangar which was just above the water level. It was a pleasant surprise to see half a dozen of Umaid Singhe's trucks waiting for us. But we were actually amazed and delighted when we found out where our 'emergency' accommodation was to be. It was to be none other than the most expensive and brand new (as it was almost completed), Chittar Palace located on the Chittar Hills to the east of the town. The Maharaja had several other palaces around the town but this was the largest and most impressive with nearly 350 rooms of every description. We were delivered in shifts to the side entrance, as you would call it of this immaculate palace. It was understandable that there was a bit of confusion initially as to just how many of us were staying and just where but overall the whole of the camp personnel, about ninety of us, were accommodated inside an hour in just one corridors worth of rooms. Although it wasn't quite finished you would hardly know it. From the outside there was a golden yellow hue about it from the type of sandstone from which it was made but there was no cement or mortar used as all the stones were joined by interlocking. There were beautiful balconies, courtyards, terraces and gardens. Inside there were different types and sizes of reception rooms, there was a music room, a proper theatre, conference rooms and an under ground swimming pool. It had several halls but the master piece was the Marwar Hall with pillars along the sides and a single arched ceiling that was highly decorated. When we met up with Josh sometime later he told us that it had taken sixteen years to build and was said to have cost £2,000,000 sterling, but this was to be our home, at least for the duration of the monsoon. To cap all of this, apart from some essential duties our time was our own!

As no vehicular traffic could get in or out of Jodhpur now, when we occasionally went into town, about three miles away we hired a Tonga. This was basically a horse and buggy type carriage, with driver. For a while the charge used to be 8 anna, but later on as more Americans came through, the charge started going up until the rate was several rupees, if they could get away with it.

Progressively, the camp was rebuilt but we had three months to wander all over the palace as well as Jodhpur town while order was reinstated and the camp was developed I think it must have been due to the floods and the damn mosquitoes but I came down with another bout of Malaria again, at this time. That was of no consequence to the other lads, some of who were getting quite familiar with some of the towns lesser known facilities. On more than one occasion I was bribed, usually with the promise of a pint, to stand on unofficial 'guard' at the bottom of some steps to an apartment, while Les looked up a 'girl' whose address he had been given, in the city. I didn't mind too much as I'd still only being married just a year and really would have liked to have seen Elsie. What with that and knowing what I was waiting for, I did feel a little uncomfortable but Les was a good mate.

One night John Elliston and I were walking back to camp from the Deoli club. We were wearing mosquito boots which had canvass tops to stop mosquitoes and scorpions getting in, when John trod on a snake. 'God', did it hiss, as both of us jumped away because neither was sure who had stood on it and there were some deadly snakes in this part of the world. We didn't know what it was at first but I was carrying my 7.62 Berretta pistol and in the half light, I could see something moving in the direction of the hissing and from the outline, it looked like a Cobra. I squeezed off a couple of rounds at the snake and it went quiet. We didn't get too close to inspect it, but it was a Cobra. Les reckoned that the flood water had probably displaced a few of them.

Another time John and I being bored and over confident went right in to the city straight through the Sojita Gate where all the shops and stalls are. I think the numerous trips we'd had with Josh might have made us a little complacent about the place. We were browsing over some stalls in a side street when we very quickly found ourselves confronted by several Ghandi supporters in their white 'forage' hats, who were obviously anti-British. They were mouthing off and shouting at us, and then were joined by a few more souls. They formed a wall across the street and would not let us pass. Then they became quite threatening and started coming towards us. The situation was getting out of hand and I was not going to have any of it. Out came the old Berretta. I held it up and cocked it then I started saying 'Chali ojow' (Hindustani for 'go away') and panned it across them. Finally we persuaded them to let us return without bother, but I think we were lucky!

One way or another, we all still went into town though. Sometimes with Josh as there was always some activity going on.

On more than one occasion, I was asked if I wanted to buy a machine gun, in the town. A machine gun was 1,000 rupees, a short magazine Lee Enfield 55 rupees, 1 anna per round of ammunition which did 'beg' a question of where the arms were coming from.

As the floods gradually receded the operational section of the camp got back in place first followed by the servicing areas and the mess. On this particular day, I was the duty Armourer and happened to be at SHQ when the duty officer came in wanting to know what staff was available. It seemed a Tigermoth had gone missing in the desert carrying a pupil pilot and a qualified pilot. This officer, Flight Lieutenant Jim Davies wanted an observer to accompany him on a search. He came over to me and said,

'We've lost an aircraft in the desert. I need someone to give me a lift to dispersal and go look for it'.

It was far better than being on guard so I offered my services.

'Good man. Come on.'

I followed him over to the equipment store where he kitted us both out with parachutes.

'Sir, I haven't done any parachuting before.'

'It's easy. All you do is keep hold of this ring, here. When you are clear of the aircraft, give it a firm pull.'

'Sir, how will I know?'

'Corporal! You stay with me. If I get out, you get out. When you're out, pull the ring and I can promise you that nobody jumps out of a completely serviceable aircraft. Is that clear?'

'Yes, Sir.'

So I acted as observer in a 4 seater Fairchild Argus which performed and sounded much better than the last airplane that I 'flew' in. Once airborne he gave me the instructions of where we were going, height and estimated arrival time. As we levelled out at about a thousand feet I settled into the co-pilots seat (starboard) as observer. It was brilliant to see aerial view of the town and the camp. I could easily follow the roads to the different palaces and my own crash site. All the horizon merged into a blue hazy strip in the far distance. After an hour or so we spotted the aircraft, nose down and tail up, not far from a railway line. We did a couple of low passes and established that the pilot was injured but the pupil was dead. Davies radioed its position and we turned back for base. He told me that a train would be sent to recover them and the aircraft and we set a course for camp. After a while Davies said to me 'take over' while he looked at the map. I had flown quite a few times before but actually being in control of a plane was a first! I managed OK, but we were a bit up and down at first. After a while I think he actually managed to read the map, with difficulty! He took the controls over and after a little while he informed me that we were to make an unscheduled stop for scientific and recreational purposes. I didn't have a clue where we were but we landed not far from a lake in a pleasantly grassed area in the middle of nowhere. We both had a smoke and took time to look at the abundant wildlife. Then we took off and returned to base! I thought to myself, 'not bad for a duty armourer'.

Considering we were at war and there was serious work to do, overall with the facilities available and the work load that was expected of us, life wasn't too bad around these parts. From the stories we heard and from the newspapers we were aware there was serious fighting going on in other places not least of all with the Japanese progressing up through Thailand and towards Burma. I don't know if Mac didn't realize or just wasn't bothered but through a basic bit of stupidity he got himself posted to Cox's Bazaar on the Burmese coast (Japanese action there), at short notice. He had stripped the cannons out of a Hurricane one day and had laid them on the bare sand for collection to the armoury. It must have been the most exceptional bit of bad luck ever but our Armourment Officer Sutherland had come by for some reason and saw fit to give him a posting for his negligence.

I didn't know any of the officers personally but you did recognize the familiar faces. I noted with some interest that a couple of weeks later, Jim Davies landed a Beaufighter, without the under carriage. He went off the runway and slid along in the sand, managing to come to rest with one wing hanging over a railway embankment. He reckoned it was a calculated soft landing with a bit of luck, perhaps! The propeller was all folded up and the undercarriage gear was all ripped and heavens knows what else, but it did fly again. I didn't actually witness the event but I saw the aircraft being recovered. I did witness a large radial engined fighter, a Vultee Vengeance come-in without undercarriage. On those, the landing gear could be operated by a handbrake type lever with a button ratchet. When the pilot got out his hand was bleeding quite badly from his efforts to operate the lever. Later on, we reckoned that he wasn't familiar with having to press the button on the lever. It needed a few repairs, a new propeller and the dents knocked out but it was OK.

As Les and I had been at some frontline operational stations we found things very quiet at Jodhpur. The working day was 8 till 5 and usually with all weekends free which left us with a bit of time to occupy ourselves. As a result almost any bright ideas for passing time were considered which could be scorpion racing, safari's (looking for lizards or anything), watching polo or any sports. Any change was welcome and with this idea in mind, it was on one of the routine start of day duties that I had an idea to make the job a little more interesting. The job was to check that the runway was serviceable and not obstructed by dead animals, impromptu camps of any other type of hazard. The Control Tower was signalled by me firing either a red or green coloured Very Pistol cartridge up in the air. Today though I thought I'd demonstrate to Les an experiment I'd been told about when I'd worked in the chemists at Worsley near Manchester, about chemicals that burn on water! I decided to fire the Very Pistol into an irrigation trench with water in to see if they floated and burned or sank and burned! This was at the end of the runway where one of the several hard standings were. I took aim pointing along the trench and downwards at about forty-five degrees. I fired. The flare shot out and hit the water and almost silently (which wasn't very impressive) bounced out again but travelled much further along the water filled trench and bounced again. We weren't going to see much at this distance now and as it hit the ground the show would be over. But it wasn't. It hit the ground and bounced many yards further along the ground only being halted by a patch of tinder dry grass which promptly started burning! That wouldn't have been too bad in isolation but the area of grass extended to the edge of the hard standing where several aircraft were parked including a Lockheed Hudson, a Vultee Vengeance, a Harvard and several bombers. As the flare travelled to its point of rest we both experienced the sickening feeling of realizing that a serious disaster was imminent. Jack and I had to race along the trench to get round to the flames and beat them like hell to put them out. We managed it, but it was touch and go whether we did or not! That was one experiment that was a bit too close for comfort, but nothing official was said! Les never let me forget it. It made me realise that even though we were doing an essential job of maintaining the armourment of the fighting aircraft, the time had come for a change of scenery and so just into December I applied for a posting to Burma, China or North West Frontier! Ten days later I was notified of my posting to Burma.

CHAPTER FIFTEEN

Up in the Hills

I took the night train from Jodhpur to Delhi and overall it wasn't a bad journey but no one would ever get a good night's sleep on it. On 23rd December I arrived in Delhi and finding the local timetable, it was with mixed feelings that I realised I had virtually all day to wait as the next train to Calcutta departed at 5 pm. I became a tourist for the day and called at the 'Red Fort' again. It's an extravagant affair with fantastic rooms and a splendid domed tower. Then I went to the 'old town' and wandered round the native bazaar with multi coloured produce of all descriptions and tea stalls. Delhi is quite a large city so there was no problem killing a few hours and after a bit of sightseeing I took a rickshaw to New Delhi and had a meal in a restaurant before going to the railway station to catch the Calcutta 'Express'. The station was really impressive from the outside as it has high straight walls interspaced with a number of castellated towers giving it the appearance of a large traditional fort. Eventually the train arrived and I was relieved to find before going there were decent carriages as I had a three day journey in front of me yet I was then somewhat apprehensive as I entered a compartment occupied by two British Army Captains of the Gurkha Regiment and a Regular Army Corporal. They seemed quite agreeable to me sharing the compartment so I shelved my bag and made myself comfortable.

Thankfully it was to be only a matter of minutes before we felt the preliminary lurching of the carriage as we pulled away which pleased everyone as air would now start circulating through the carriages. My arrangements were looking quite good so far but there was still a task in hand, namely to travel three days with two Army Gurkha Captains. But even that was soon eliminated as after an hour or so the Captains had made light conversation between themselves and I fancied a meander up the train. As officers are all ways I/C of the room I stood up and said 'Permission to leave the room Sir?'

Both Captains looked at each other then back at me.

'Airman.' one of them said. 'There is a war on. We've all got a job to do but we are going to be on this train for nearly three days. I think it would be in order to relax formalities for the duration. What do you say?'

'Yes Sir. Fine by me Sir.'

'And you Corporal? You OK with that?'

'Fine, Sir.'

'Excellent. I'm Clive Jackson and this is Dave Huntcliffe.' he paused. 'Well, carry on then.'

We continued to roll through plains of fields, sometimes marshes and sometimes scrub heading down to Calcutta. The corporal was called Dave and we chatted on and off as matters of interest arose. After 24 hours the two Captains opened a Christmas hamper which was a hamper and a half. It was full of luxury goodies and things like different cheeses, tins of fruit and different meats, most of which I hadn't heard of, and a bottle of rum. It was wonderful just to look at but when Dave and I were invited to partake of the contents and the rum, it really did seem like Christmas. The short bread of all things was just the same as my last Christmas at the Commercial when half the furniture was pushed back to allow the table to open up for Christmas dinner. With mum and dad, Llewi and Mary, Elsie and her mother that visited. The fire would be made up and the smell of roast dinner filled the air with the faithful decorations struggling to glimmer. It was a very warm feeling of home and seemed a long way distant. Before the war, I would never have imagined that I'd spend Christmas with a couple of Gurkha Officers and a hamper on a train in the middle of India! It was difficult to make such a boring train journey interesting but we did what we could, which wasn't very much.

We arrived at Howrah Station, Calcutta at 1600 hrs Christmas Day 1943. As we approached the outskirts of Calcutta the train slowed down and I put my head outside the window for a look around as the surrounding fields gave way to various shacks with buildings and yards housing all sorts of industry and animals. As we got to the city I saw a number of dead being carried through the streets, many in an upright position. It turned out that roads and railways to Arakan had been destroyed as part of a political revolt against the British Government as a result of the Cripps Mission it had prevented food and goods being transported to their own people in the towns creating a famine. As Howrah Station approached other trains were waiting to depart with carriages full of people and their produce not only inside but on the roof and clinging to the outsides as well. It seemed a rather a dodgy practice and a moment later I was proved right as we passed a blood stained turban with a body next to it. I guess one of them had lost his grip but no one seemed unduly concerned. The train finally stopped and as we got out many Indians filled the train both inside and out. Dave and I bid the Captains farewell and then said cheerio to each other. It was late afternoon on Christmas day and though clearly I knew where I was, I didn't know anyone else here and I didn't know where anything else was. All I knew was that I had to catch the night train for Burma and Dimapur in about 5 hours. As I left the station and waited in Chowringhee, the main street to get my bearings, by chance met Dave again.

We both felt a little awkward at having said cheerio just ten minutes earlier but restarted our conversation. Neither of us had been to Calcutta before nor had much money to spend. We didn't have anywhere to go or time to do anything else so for four rupees between us we bought ourselves a Christmas present of a bottle of Carrews Gin. We drank it sitting on the steps of Howrah Railway Station just talking whilst being quietly amazed at the vast array of cycles and rickshaws, people and mules passing by. After a couple of hours Dave got his train to Chittagong, just round the coast a bit and we parted company for the last time. Eventually my train to Burma arrived which slightly wobbly, I boarded. I didn't have much problem getting some sleep and woke up hours later as we approached the ferry crossing of the vast Brahmaputra River where we all had to leave the train to cross the river by the ferry which took two to three hundred people at a time. Once on the other side we boarded another train to Dimapur which after a few hours started to climb steadily from the valley of the river and wind its way up into the hills. After only a few hours we arrived at Dimapur station, right in the hills where the railway then disappeared in to the outer reaches of the Himalayas in the distance. It was late evening on Boxing Day. The transit camp was only a short distance away where I reported in and was allocated a place on the next convoy to Imphal which was to be the following day. If the weather was good and we didn't have any serious problems it would be two days at least but that could easily be three or even four. It was quite a busy camp as everything no matter what it was had to be shifted either from train to truck or truck to train. I found the mess and got some food before finding a bed space. I ended up talking with an MT sergeant over a 'tea' and a couple of smokes.

The following morning I joined the convoy of about twenty-five Chevrolet '3 tonners' with a full two days travelling ahead. 130 miles of jungle and mountains lay ahead by way of Kohima, a small garrison town which was about seventy miles from Imphal. To talk about a road, was an overstatement as it was barely more than a single track that had been metalled some time ago. It sought its perilous way for about fifty miles over, around and between the mountains and on to Kohima sitting high in the mountains. From the depths of ravines to the edge of shear drops hundreds of feet below, the road wound its wearisome way through the mountains. I couldn't help thinking back to driving the hippo (fuel tanker) around some of the more remote areas of Lancashire. Some of the roads we had to visit then were a bit rough and remote but compared to now, they seemed like pristine A roads. It had come about that all the Brit's convoys used native drivers. Something to do with it being a bit of an insult if the Indian drivers weren't good enough to drive our convoys.

The convoys ran quite frequently but at irregular times and were called 'L of C's' (Lines of Communication) usually taking much needed supplies in to the Imphal plain and bringing wounded, sick or personnel with changed orders, out. It was a very bad road with many long snake-passes both up and down where the only difference was it was wet and muddy in the valleys and dry and crumbling on the hills. All over it was jungle. Lower down there were some passing places in the valleys where the vegetation was thick and the air very humid. Both the air and the vegetation thinned as the altitude increased up to the craggy mountains covered with gnarled rocky crests. To get over the mountains there were countless hairpin bends to the extent that sometimes we would do five miles travelling to get one mile in distance. On the first day, an Indian Air Force chap leaned out of the window and lost his cap. The road was so narrow that as he leaned further out looking for it he fell out of the truck and was immediately falling down a near vertical incline. The convoy stopped, but when others got to him, it was very obvious that the bloke was dead.

The other Hindus made a funeral pyre and cremated him. It was a nightmare of a journey as most times we were crawling along just trying to stay on the road, it was hot, uncomfortable, noisy and very humid and this carried on into the night as the drivers changed but that did not give the rest of us any respite as any idea of sleep was impossible. The convoy continued on to Kohima, at 5,000 ft above sea level, which was an Army staging post and transit camp run by a Regimental Sergeant Major. There we had a serve yourself breakfast, then continued the next seventy miles to Imphal. All convoys used the same route.

At particularly bad (treacherous) bends along the route now and again a truck would go over the edge, maybe a 1,000 ft below, being wrecked with others who had made a similar mistake. In effect there were grave yards of trucks at the more notorious points of the route. Nearer Imphal, there was a clearing where maybe 200 trucks that had been recovered were stored. This told us that we were getting near to Imphal and sure enough, after a dozen or so more bends, the town came in to view. No one cared what it actually looked like as it signified an end to the arse ache, the back ache and the dull monotonous modulation of the engines. We were so pleased to see it, we thought it was beautiful. It was certainly smaller than Jodhpur but seemed more civilised. I don't know that it was, but probably seemed like it due to nearly all the houses and buildings in the town having large roofs of red tiles. The town was formed out of a cluster of Naga villages amidst plantain and bamboo groves. The buildings weren't very high only two or three storeys with a common market place and small narrow roads in-between.

The camp was located just outside of the town at the northern most point of the vast Imphal Plain. It was a plain indeed but its appearance was most deceptive and technically it was a valley and certainly did not reveal the rare combination of attributes that created such a geographical jewel. As we stopped it was obvious that nearly all the camp was either tented or had native bamboo and mud huts with sandy tracks in-between as accommodation, which seemed alright but I wondered how water proof they were because it never just rained here it was usually torrential. I found the SHQ to join 28 Sqdn on 30 December. I had my arrival chit signed then I was told to find a 'Basha' (hut) and report to the armoury. The whole squadron had only been here since the end of October so although things were a little 'ad hock' at times they were certainly not relaxed as I was put on duty straight away working on Hurricane IIb's.

CHAPTER SIXTEEN

The Imphal Valley

It only took a couple of days to get the picture of where we were and why. The whole area was a large narrow and fertile plain about twenty-five miles by five or six miles and was 2,500 ft above sea level located only a few miles from the border with Burma and for at least two hundred miles in any direction there were mountains up to 9,000 ft high all around. To the east was the Barail Range of mountains, to the north and east were the Naga Hills, to the south were the Chin Hills with the rugged jungle covered mountains of Burma to the east and the south. The plain itself was full of diversity as basically it was a huge valley into which several rivers from the surrounding hills drained and the lush green vegetation promoted a variety of wildlife from water buffalo in the south and deer throughout the valley down to an infinite number of crawling things that could literally get anywhere and then bite. Throughout the forests generally there were small monkeys to be found and in the hilly districts Hoolock Gibbons were known to live with leopards being natural predators in the remote areas. Further north above the Imphal valley the Himalayan Black Bear lived in the foothills of the vast mountain range. In the north of the Imphal valley, the town sat on raised ground with the Manipur River on the eastern side. To the south of the valley the road wound its way south and up through the hills to Tiddim at an elevation of 8,000 ft above sea level. Further along the road the border was crossed into Burma and on to Mandalay but it was often unserviceable in the rains. To the east, there was an oxen track over the hills to Silchar and Patharkandi in the west but it too was only passable in dry weather and the same applied to the couple of tracks eastwards into Burma. Much of the valley was extensive farming land with the occasional hillock here and there and travelling through it the mountains on both sides were always domineering. To the east and south the land was very marshy with lots of pools which developed in the south to form Loktak Lake. For some years now Imphal, with an airfield just outside (now our camp), had been an established forward base for operations in South East Asia.

Geographically the plain was a strategic oasis amongst thousands of square miles of mountainous terrain which formed the immense natural barrier between India, China and Burma with the only road between them traversing the plain. This was the valley that had to be held at all costs against the Japanese because as they advanced into Burma, Imphal became the gateway to India and the most strategic position in South East Asia and therefore, one of their key objectives. Due to this fact the Allied forces had built six new airstrips with Imphal and Kangala further north, Wangjing central and Bishenpur to the west leaving Palel at the south near Sapam. The roads and tracks had been improved for lines of communication and fuel and ammunition dumps established.

There was a great deal of activity going on with Dakotas and Curtiss Commandos (C46) operating from Imphal and Palel constantly bringing supplies in throughout the day and leaving with wounded servicemen and civilians.

The fighter squadrons had two key roles one being to protect the transport aircraft in the local area and the other was to attack the enemy as and when required as army support. As a result the work of the ground crew was round the clock as the servicing was done at night wherever possible to leave the aircraft armed and ready for service the following day. All of this was in pretty sharp contrast to life at Jodhpur, with the exception of the mosquitoes and Malaria, but this is what the frontline troops needed and we were the key support that enabled it to happen. The threat of attack was constantly with us as well because there were various reports of Japanese advance parties penetrating right into the plain to cause disruption and report observations. One day I watched a Hurricane as it was shot down maybe a mile or so away. He made a safe landing just into the hills then the pilot got out then set fire to the aircraft.

You could easily see that he hadn't gone down very far away at all, but the pilot was never seen again.

I'd only been there a couple of weeks when it 'became known' that the Japanese were to mount an attack to the south west of the plain. We kept hearing spurious reports from the pilots of numbers and positions but it all boiled down to a hell of a lot of Japanese troops accumulating, we didn't know just when but there'd be no mistake when it started. As things were though neither pilots nor armourers could work non stop and there were occasions when we were stood down for a few hours. It was then a few of us would head off in to Imphal town. A lot of the people had been evacuated but there was still something of a market there with fresh produce to supplement a diet of dehydrated foods. The people were different and usually pleased to see us but sometimes I think they wanted to see our money as well. In any event it was a pleasant change as the alternative was to eat which was a poor option, sleep which was very difficult or work which we did the remainder of the time. I had only been there just a month and then I received a posting to 5 Squadron on 1 February down to the southern end of the plain at Sapam about five miles north of Palel. This was nothing out of the ordinary as with sickness, injury and movements, staff were constantly changing to maintain service requirements. I only had my basic kit to get together then got a lift with one of six trucks taking supplies and ammunition to the outlying airstrips. On the twenty-eight mile journey we kept passing different trucks of battle weary soldiers returning from the frontline to the south, most of which seemed in a bad way but not demoralized as we were getting the usual sort of banter from them. Some of the comments did give food for thought though which basically boiled down to 'what the hell did we think we were going to do with six truck loads of supplies against a Japanese Division that's waiting just over the hill?' We didn't have an answer but we didn't have a lot of time either so on we pressed to Sapam. We had been told that only pockets of twenty or so Japanese troops were breaking through in isolated places but the truth was there were two Japanese divisions heading towards us as the attack had started on the Arakan, the area just south of us.

We arrived at the airfield and I reported in at HQ, Sqdn Ldr. Sharp was Officer I/C 5 Sqdn. It was mostly tented accommodation with some 'bashas' and a single large marquee as the mess. It was a fairly basic airstrip just out from Sapam village with a single runway sitting in a sort of 'bay' of the valley formed by the line of scrub and trees which rose into the hills, not too far away. There were two or three squadrons including No. 8 Indian Squadron and No.1, both with Vultee Vengeance dive bombers from RIAF.

At Sapam, in addition to doing the usual armourers jobs as I was at Imphal, I was put in charge of the armourers on 'B' Flight which had seven aircraft. My job was to make sure the aircraft were refuelled and rearmed as required. This involved attending at the pilots debrief after any mission to find out the state of the guns, how much ammunition was used, the mixture desirability and find any problems etc. Myself, a Corporal, Dave Peacock LAC and Bill Cranston A/C Hand, were responsible for aircraft armoury servicing usually it was at 50 hours and 100 hours. Part of the job was to remove 4 x 20 mm. Hispano cannons from the aircraft then dismantle, inspect and check the mechanism and bore with gauges then refit and harmonize the gun sights. Corporal Sanderson was an armourer I/C 'A' Flight. He was a Scotsman and was known as Sand the Scot because his name got confused with Cpl. Anderson.

On 7 March the Japanese launched another attack, this time with Tiddim as the objective which was just down the road from us and we could hear some of the action taking place. Just over a hill was a valley where some Japanese became dug into positions on either side in the hills facing each other and this made direct attacks on their positions quite difficult and hazardous. That's when we were really kept on our toes! No effort was spared to support our troops and to reach the objectives. To this ends, an unofficial bomb was produced. We used the Hurricane long distance fuel tanks (45 gallons of fuel each side) and then connected a Mills bomb, a No. 36 Hand grenade to each one. The tanks were then jettisoned by the fighters over the dug-in Japanese (the bunkers), with the grenade attached which became armed as the tanks were dropped from the aircraft. Whenever engagements were in progress aircraft were constantly returning to be re-armed before taking off again. Each day box after box of ammunition was emptied as the fighters did what they could and each night the guns would be checked along with the magazines, then serviced and set up again if needed. We didn't need any Commanders to tell us there was a lot of action taking place. The Japanese kept coming for a few days but were repulsed by the Indian Army. The pressure then eased off for a while.

After dark there was usually a camp fire as a source of light and a focal point. At any time any of the staff be they commissioned or non-commissioned would be sat around it chatting and smoking or having a drink and exchanging stories as there were few alternatives to hand. Squadron Leader Sharp occasionally came up with a further option in the form of one of his 'lectures'.

7. *A Hawker Hurricane Mk.IIb receiving an overhaul. Copyright of Imperial War Museum.*

He was an ex 'Wingate Expedition' man and sometimes he gave lectures with slides of the expedition, showing what a hard slog it was. How dense and difficult the jungle really was and how only mules could be used for moving equipment. He explained how our 'Chindits' worked behind enemy lines causing disruption and reporting movements and often engaged the enemy. Due to the remote and extreme conditions they operated in, the walking wounded were OK but otherwise they were shot as it was impossible for the expedition to carry any wounded and it was impossible for any wounded to survive on their own. I suppose overall they were morale boosting, as afterwards each man was resolved to 'getting it right'. Another time a group of us were having a chat when Dave Peacock told us about a bit of a hairy incident when he had been an armourer on an aircraft carrier with Sea Hawks on board, before he remustered to the RAF. Whilst he was in the cockpit of an aircraft he was servicing on the deck a mishap occurred which resulted in making the aircraft under carriage collapse. As this threw Dave forward with his hands in front of him for protection he unavoidably pressed the 'fire' button for the guns resulting in a burst of cannon fire right across the deck. It was certainly impressive to hear but I made a mental note to double check any trestles I used in future! I had a little sympathy with 'Sand the Scots' particular experience of a clearing rod as only an armourer would ever come across this and I remembered what we were told in training. He had been required to use one for a lodged shell in a gun barrel and the thing exploded. He told us that it shot out of the barrel like a bullet, went clean through the fuselage of an aircraft, straight through the side of a truck and came to rest in a piano in the crew room after going through the wall! In addition to this as the gun breech was open the blast had seriously damaged part of the wing. The inauspicious clearing rod.

During March Sapam became nigh on isolated as we were told that the entire valley was now under siege, that's when I along with 5 Sqdn ground crew, was moved to separate accommodation in the village huts with Naga Tribesmen. At about the same time we heard that the Japanese had 'taken' the main Burma Road in two places, one at Kohima Pass about ninety miles north of the valley and at Tiddim (at 8,000 ft) a few miles to the south of the valley and this virtually isolated the Imphal plain with the exception of the fair weather track to Silchar. The whole situation was looking just about as serious as it gets. The Jap 33rd Divn had advanced to the south of Tiddim cutting off the Indian 17 Divn. It was touch and go for a week or so but they managed to withdraw to the plain with help from the army and air support. As the whole valley was under siege by the Japanese the entire conflict was now totally dependant on air support. Our 'Flight' was conducting up to thirty-two sorties a day. That in turn determined a working day could be up to 20 or 30 hours long on servicing or repair, after which we would be given the afternoon off! During this time there the heavy transport aircraft were flying endless sorties bringing supplies troops and equipment in and evacuating sick and injured personnel out. It must have been hell for the troops in the jungle and we weren't 'clear' of any action either as the Japanese wanted control of the valley. Many a time we came under fire from the occasional shell and mortars.

The mess at Sapam was a huge marquee and as it was a frontline airfield anyone sat anywhere, including non-commissioned with commissioned and as you entered, there hung the score board with the daily and weekly tally of hits on it. Anything the fighters got was put up, vehicles, mules, elephants, supplies or anything. The food there was more or less the same as at Imphal, hard tack biscuits and dehydrated onions which could be mixed together into a sort of porridge for breakfast but I hated onions and always have done. I soon realized you have to be extremely hungry to eat something you really don't like. Often there would be 7 lb. tins of Olio margarine with a slice of bread, goat's cheese, jam or any combination thereof. One of the favourites and most frequent was tinned Soya Link sausages. They were 99% Soya bean and did taste a bit like sausages if they were well done. Sometimes they were served at breakfast and the cooks used to improve them by serving them with jam to give them some flavour but there were thirty ways of serving corned beef and dehydrated potatoes for dinner. Sometimes there was marmalade on the table with bread and Ghee butter which turned to oil in the heat.

All around the place there were rats scavenging for food, they didn't live naturally in the jungle but there wasn't an airfield in the valley that didn't have them. Occasionally aircrew would borrow a shotgun from the armoury and see what game they could pot at the edge of the jungle for a bit of rest and relaxation, we were told. Being an armourer that didn't seem a bad idea to me and as I could sign a shotgun out as well, so sometimes I did the same. One day I was out 'hunting' and became really pleased with myself when I managed to bag a couple of pigeons. As food was always in short supply I was determined to eat them so I roughly plucked them, then encased them in clay, made a fire and cooked them. As they were cooking I found myself looking into the same fire as when my old school friend Frank Aberton and I were camping out in his back garden. He must have been a good friend as that was only a few days after another school friend, Donald Buckland and I had tied poor Frank up and rolled him in to the river, like mates do. He was alright about it but his mother gave us a right 'ear bashing'. Suddenly I was aware that I'd lost track of time and was concerned about my dinner. I flipped both clay lumps out of the fire and opened them up. They smelled beautiful and I took great relish in eating them freshly cooked and hot. They were delicious.

The isolation of the airfield and the proximity of the Japanese produced a very close knit unit. From the mess point of view it wasn't all bad news as due to some resourceful fitters occasionally additional supplies were available. This was done by means of long range wing tanks on the Hurricanes being modified so that the domed front end of the tank was removed then a few of the baffles inside of the tank removed and the domed front end fitted back. The extra rations were delivered to the 'Naafi' where they were distributed. Sometimes there was a beer ration which created a standard saying of 'three bottles per man perhaps'. A popular favourite because it was most frequent was 'Pure Old Panther Piss' an Assam brew but only the Sergeants Mess had a spirit ration, it didn't mean we couldn't drink any though!

As and when supplies available the Sergeants and upwards would be drinking Prince Calvert Whiskey and Canadian Club in the evening either round the fire or in the mess. More often than not a Sergeant would come round, sometimes close together in time, to the ground crew in their tents or 'bashas' with a bottle of something and used to half fill our tin mugs. If someone did not want it for any reason, he would be tipped out of his charpoy. The rum that came round was thick and black like Molasses and usually accompanied by Sergeant

Abraham who was about 6ft medium build and just about bald, he was a bit of a mouthy sod, but he was a fair man. He would come round our tents or huts with the rum ration and demand that everyone sing, by singing himself 'sing, sing you bastards sing, or I'll snatch your ring,' meaning with his boot! On such an evening I was in our 'basha' with Bill quite a bit later in the night. We were both having a drink and a smoke, each laid on a charpoy. As it was night time and really quiet any sound travelled really well. As we were chatting I kept hearing something rustling not far away but I couldn't make it out. I asked Bill about it but he said he couldn't hear anything but I was sure I kept hearing something. I didn't say anything to Bill but if it was a Japanese ambush, I wasn't going to investigate and be the first one they shot. So I thought I'd let them go round our basha then get them from behind. Bill didn't seem concerned, which worried me. Then I clearly heard the snap of a twig, then I heard a squeak and a shuffling in the roof. It was a bloody rat! I was relieved that it wasn't an ambush but I was so annoyed a rat had put the frighteners on me I just took my issue .45 Thompson machine gun and in the process of silencing the rat, blasted 'a bloody great hole in the roof'. Bill just shook his head amid a shower of dust and debris that came floating down and said 'A bit excessive old boy'. He looked at his drink then added 'and if I had wanted a straw, I'd have asked for one. OK?' as he pulled a piece of straw thatch from his drink.

One day a plane spotted loads of Japanese troops caught in open ground as part of their movements to strengthen their lines. An observer radioed their position then every available squadron was alerted. They were given the co-ordinates and ordered to straff and bomb the area. After a couple of hours hundreds of Japanese were either dead or wounded. The mess tally board got a bit of a boost on that day. Aircraftman Weston got a boost of a different sort that day also as one of our Flights aircraft returned not having used any ammunition and at the debrief the pilot reported 'all four guns not working'. This was very serious when you're up against the enemy so I made a point of checking it myself. I went over to the aircraft and climbed on the wing, opened the panel and found all four breach blocks along side the guns in the wings had not been reassembled after inspection. I was fuming mad as the negligence could have cost lives and possibly an aircraft as well. I discovered it was Aircraftman Weston who had prepared the guns so I found him out and got him on the wing and showed him. He knew he was in serious trouble and he also knew there was nothing he could say by way of excuse. I told him to stand up and face me. I said 'do you want a court marshal or will you take my punishment?' (words I'd heard before). Everybody knew that the CO had been one of Wingates Men. Weston said 'yours'. I socked Weston under the chin knocking him off the wing and into the mud. I reported 'over-size ammunition' and knew full well that he'd never make the same mistake again.

When I looked over our cluster of Hurricanes there seemed little to be impressed about. They were all dirty with oil and coolant stains about them, there were patches here and there from bullets and shrapnel. There was nothing to indicate the power they harboured or the speed and precision by which they operated. The young pilots might seem somewhat blase about them but they all flew those planes with their souls and used everything they knew and did all they could to achieve their objectives. Aircraft often returned with twigs and branches snagged in parts of the wings and wheels which was a good indication of the type of flying they were doing especially when under fire but no one could refute one pilot's complaint about the way it handled. When the aircraft was checked out the problem was identified as Japanese barbed wire that was snagged around the tail wheel!

Due to the advance of the Japanese, to the south of the valley on 20 March our domestic site with the squadron's equipment was 'boxed'. This was a defence strategy whereby all the equipment and anything available was used to create a square barrier around personnel and essential equipment. Anything that moved outside of the 'box', unless otherwise notified, was the enemy and dealt with appropriately. We could hear action taking place in the hills around us and on a few occasions we were directly targeted ourselves. One chap from the ground crew had a Japanese bullet, (ball ammunition) hit his pillow during a daytime raid, the bloke wasn't in bed but he must have had some thoughts about it as it was probably fired over a mile away. That night one chap coming off guard duty got virtually cut in two by some other guard getting 'touchy'. There was a lot of tension about so I didn't have any reservations about having to bollock an Indian guard who was cleaning a Sten gun with the magazine still in it. Stens had a very heavy breach block and a very light creep spring. It didn't take much to make it fire and we needed all the ammunition and men that we could muster! As the extent of the offensive became clear it became known that two Japanese Divisions were heading for the south of the valley and one was heading for a pass on the main supply route in the north at Kohima.

On 23 March our squadron was given forty-five minutes notice to break camp. We had to prepare all the twelve serviceable aircraft we had to be flown to Silchar as all unserviceable aircraft were to be destroyed along with village and everything else. Then we had to make sure that anything explosible and burnable was grouped together so the Royal Engineers could burn the Naga village due to the Japanese being about ten miles away. The most anyone left with was the clothes on their back and maybe a small kitbag.

CHAPTER SEVENTEEN
The long way Home

All of us ground crew required for operational duties were then taken in trucks to Palel where three American Curtis Commando's were waiting. There was no messing about as we were off the trucks and on the planes in minutes as the last man 'took out' each of the trucks with a grenade. As we were taking off, the Japanese had managed to set up an artillery piece and we came under fire as we taxied! We all flew on to Silchar about ninety miles over the hills to the west. The remaining personnel not required for operational flying duties were relocated to strengthen another forward airfield at Wangjing.

In those first six weeks I was told later that thirty-two aircraft had been lost and six pilots were missing.

The aircraft that myself and the flight support crew were in landed at an airfield in the foothills of the Barail Mountains not far from Silchar, along with the Hurricanes from Palal. A couple of other squadrons were already there including 615 and 60. It was only then that we were invited to inspect the damage to one of the C46s we had been in. Low down on the starboard side of the fuselage, a little behind the wing was a very neat hole about two inches in diameter and on the port side of the fuselage quite high up was another hole about two inches in diameter. A shell had gone straight through the fuselage of the plane in front of us on take off! There were a few raised eyebrows but 'a miss is a miss' wherever you are and as we all had work to do we were directed to find our quarters then loosely put into groups to work on servicing the aircraft. The airfield was a mile or two from the town itself which was nestled within a large loop of the Bara River. Both the town and the river was large enough to support a small port which allowed trading up and down the river which was bordered by plots of fields but the arable ground soon gave way to thick wild vegetation and jungle leading into the hills all around. From March to October the climate was very tropical being very hot and very humid with a heavy rainfall and frequent violent thunderstorms.

This was the height of the battle of Imphal with fierce fighting taking place as the Japanese were totally desperate to break through where ever they could.

Within a couple of days a few of us including myself were posted to a Repair and Salvage Unit at Patharkandi, a few miles from Silchar but still in the Sylhet District 'for a month or two'. Officially our squadron was formally operating from a forward airfield at Wangjing in the Imphal valley but flew in there from Patharkandi and Silchar.

At this time there was fierce fighting taking place both at the south on the Tiddim Road and in the north just into the hills at Kohima which dominated the main supply route into the valley. There we had a Regiment of the Royal West Kents with a Company of 7 Rajput Regiment and a few troops from other Indian Regiments that had become isolated there and the word was that our lads were holding out against a whole division of Japanese.

As we arrived at Patharkandi airfield we reported in to a large 'basha'. We were simply asked our name and trade. I promptly said 'Butterworth' and made a point of saying 'Armourer, I/C B Flight, Sapam.' The Sergeant in front of me sharply called out 'Bert', 'I've got you an Armourer.' Bert, a Chief Technician put his head round the doorway removing his pipe and said 'Right, we've got pre flight inspections. Come on!' I went out with him to find Steve an Engine Fitter waiting with a young looking Aircraft Hand, in this case our driver and we proceeded to find a Chevy truck. We were headed for one of the farther dispersals nearly two miles from the domestic site. There was nothing impressive about the truck but it was quite refreshing to travel at twenty to thirty mph in the oppressive 95° midday heat. We knew we were getting close to 'our' dispersal because there was only jungle beyond it. But we didn't quite get close enough. About 200 yds from nearest Hurricane the truck started to misfire and jerk quite distinctly. Our driver did a good job of coaxing it further while Chiefy was cursing 'so and so' American crap. I did think it was somewhat unjustified considering we'd just been flown out of 'the valley' in American aircraft, by American pilots and under fire but none of that helped. We stopped about thirty yards short. Now we did have a predicament although Chiefy had calmed down a bit and accepted the situation. We could start the 'pre-flight inspections' but equally we were isolated at the edge of the jungle and quite open to rogue Japanese scouting parties. That was not a good situation to be in. The alternative was for 'someone' to walk back to camp in the intense heat and get a lift back with some fuel. No one wanted the walk back and no one was keen to remain so vulnerable with the aircraft. Collectively we were open to ideas but none were forth coming until Chiefy pointed out that we were thirty yards from about 90 gallons of fuel, indicating the nearest Hurricane. Three pairs of eyes lit up as the idea registered but we still had to transfer two or three gallons of fuel over thirty yards with no equipment. Chiefy was thinking about this until his raised eyebrows registered a decision.

'Right.' he said. 'We are going to refuel this truck from that aircraft. I will open the wing tank drain valve in the cockpit while you three collect the fuel in your bush hats and quickly transfer it to the truck.'

It was a fact that we all had bush hats but it was equally true that they were old, used and well creased. Chiefy may have realised this but at the same time there was nothing else.

'When you are in position with your hat, you will shout 'On' and when it is full you will shout 'Off'. Is that clear?' There was a unison of 'Yes Chief.'

'Driver. You remove the truck filler cap.'

'Yes Chief.'

'Steve, you're first, get in position.' Steve crouched under the wing with the bowl of his hat in position.

'You two get ready with your hats.'

'Yes Chief.' With that, Chiefy leaned over into the cockpit to reach the fuel drain valve.

'Ready?' he shouted from up top.

'On.' With that fuel gushed out of the orifice in the wing and filled Steve's hat in two seconds. Immediately Steve shouted 'Off.' but not before a couple of surplus pints had flooded on to the floor. He promptly got up and headed for the truck. In the intense sunlight all the miniscule droplets of fuel that fell from and filtered through the hat on the thirty-yard trip burst into resplendent colours as the brilliant sunlight was refracted through them. He got to the truck and managed to pour some into the tank. It wasn't a lot though.

'Come on Butterworth. Next.' I proceeded to repeat the operation and by shouting 'Off' almost straight away managed to get only a pint or so of excess fuel. An improvement. I arrived at the truck with maybe three quarters of a hat full and probably got more than half a hat full in the tank. And so the sequence of events continued until Chiefy estimated the amount of fuel in the tank to be two gallons. It was very hot work in the heat of the day and seemed to take ages but it might have been fifteen minutes or so.

'Right. Well done lads. That'll do.' The pressure was off and we relaxed looking forward to a drink when we got back. Chiefy closed the cockpit and got down as the driver went round to get in the truck and start the engine while we waited for Chiefy before getting in ourselves. It was only a few seconds later, maybe six or eight that we then heard a desperate cry from the other side of the truck of 'Chiefy! Fire! Fire!'

This was a 'bolt out of the blue' but we stepped forward from the truck to see a line of thick yellow flame travelling towards the Hurricane at a good rate of knots. We also saw Chiefy desperately stamping around in front of it trying to stop its advance. It went straight past him as the path was too wide and it stopped at the largest wet patch of fuel under the aircraft wing where it instantly flared up. At this point we knew the aircraft was a 'goner' but there was still fuel on board and magazines of ammunition. We couldn't do anything about the fuel but the ammunition belts could be removed in seconds. There was good reason to remove them if at all possible as when they exploded the shells would go in random directions and possibly kill us as well. I set off at once for the plane and took a running jump on to the wing even as the flames were starting to come through. I took the panel off and released the ammo belts and just threw them somewhere clear then I went round to the other side and did the same then got as far away as I could. To one side of me I saw three other figures desperately running as well which was understandable as the truck now had flames all around it and those fuel tanks were about to explode! We were a few hundred yards away when it went up. There was a terrific roar as a great fireball of dirty yellow flame rose up surrounded by thick black smoke, just like at Jodhpur. There were mixed feelings as we just stood and watched. The atmosphere was soon given direction.

'And what the flaming hell happened there?' Chiefy now had an extremely demanding tone!

He scanned all of us for a response. 'Dunno Chief.' replied Steve.

As I received his glare I replied 'Don't know Chief.' When our driver was targeted Chiefy was quick to add 'If those two don't know anything, I guess you do!'

The LAC was so nervous he could hardly speak. 'Well!' he demanded. Chiefy was merciless in getting the LAC to account for his actions and assured him that he hadn't heard the end if it. It seems the LAC hadn't been sure whether the manual fuel valve under the seat had been turned off or not and to save getting a flat battery he went to check. As we had all been in glaring sunshine he couldn't see in the shade of the truck so he had lit a match to see the position. That itself didn't cause a problem but when it burnt down to his finger he dropped it which did cause a problem! Chiefy wasn't happy at all but neither were we as all of us now had a two mile trek back to camp across the open airfield in the heat of the day and there was an aircraft to account for! We set off for camp in an awkward mutual silence as each of us contemplated the trouble that now awaited our return. After a short time our silent trek was interrupted by Chiefy demonstrating some peculiar behaviour. It looked like he was trying to catch something running round his body. He then stopped and looked rather sick. 'Where's my frigging pipe?' he demanded. He may have been talking to us or to God himself because I think he was hoping for a miracle. Even if one of us had got his pipe, no one would have admitted it as I'm sure they would have been killed! Steve cautiously prompted that he had it with him in the truck, to which Chiefy agreed, and looked worried then added something about fuel valves, then proceeded to swear profusely. We continued our trek in silence with the LAC some distance behind. We all realised that his pipe may have been in the aircraft, or, it may still be on the ground nearby waiting to be found! Nearer camp he made a point of telling us that he would be making a report of the incident, that it was his report and that we were to keep quiet about it. Did we really understand!

The next day a general alert was issued due to Japanese activity reported in the vicinity.

This wasn't too fabricated in reality as the Japanese were advancing round the southern end of the valley.

A couple of days or so later a replacement Hurricane arrived from the stock replacement aircraft (as we were the MU, otherwise it would have taken a while longer to be flown out), it was an ex Battle of Britain Mk. V and had just received its second major overhaul. On 27 March about lunchtime Flt.Lt. Lee who had over 9,000 hours flying time logged, took the replacement aircraft up for an A & E (airframe and engine) test flight. As an experienced pilot he could check out the handling of the aircraft and feel how it responded and performed.

On the same day myself with a bunch of armourers were coming from the mess after lunch and were making our way to the armoury when we heard, a Merlin engine, quite high up going flat out. We searched the area of sky really hard only to see a Hurricane in a power dive. It just kept getting steeper and steeper until it was near vertical and flat out at around 400 mph with the super charger at a screaming pitch. There was a ghostly aspect to the spectacle as we could see right through it as almost like a skeleton it powered right into the ground and exploded less than fifty yards away with such a heart stopping thud we felt the impact through our feet and watched a wall of earth and debris rise and fall then silence. When we realised there were no after effects we ran to the edge of what was really a crater the size of a large living room and just stared, looking for something we recognised. All that was to be seen was half a landing wheel and a cannon sticking straight up at the bottom. It was later discovered that the skin material had stripped off the airframe because it was rotten. A few of us proved this to ourselves when we found a piece of the tail material with the No. on it and one of the airframe lads told us of the patch test from training, where a two inch circle of material was removed and folded in half. If it folded over without cracking the material was good. The piece we tried didn't get half way before cracking. It was evident that the material had stripped of the wing which had exposed the inner wing compartments and then the fuselage to a terrific air pressure which must have blown the rest of the skin off, from the inside out in seconds. Nearby we found the wing panel covers. Another replacement was ordered.

About 1 or 2 April the Wangjing section of 5 Sqdn moved to Lanka which was a good way north of Imphal and joined the Patharkandi section which had moved there on 29 March. This was most probably for no lesser reason than the Japanese being reported as only ten miles from Imphal. This left a detachment of us including myself operating the Repair and Salvage Unit. Aircraft would come in for all sorts of repairs to keep them flying and firing. We might be cannibalising parts, harmonizing guns or repairing shell damage, we were very busy. During this time it was the availability of different airfields in the area that enabled the fighters to continue operations without being too far away from the enemy. The Japanese were driving really hard wherever they could but our troops were relatively fresh and in good spirits.

There were serious losses, even though we were holding our own, by day all of us would be listening from any available source of news of how our lads were getting on. The fact that we had been posted out of the valley (the gateway to India) was dire in itself but there were thousands of troops still fighting there and equipment and men were constantly being flown in. We just had to match the Japanese and hold them. The pinnacle of this defence happened in April when the Royal West Kents with the company of 7 Rajput Regiment and other Indian troops held out under seige for three weeks against 12,000 Japanese. We heard that they had been relieved, Kohima had been held and the Japanese advance had been checked. This was a turning point but it was at great cost. It was later revealed that during this period Transport Command flew in 12,500 troops, 18,800 tons supplies and flew out 13,000 casualties and 43,000 non combatants.

Green 'V' cigarettes were issued but they were so rough that even some of the natives wouldn't smoke them! I stuck to my Cheroot cigars but even these weren't enough to keep the mosquitoes at bay as almost straight away I went down with malaria again. The river being not far away and the vegetation and extreme humidity created a breeding ground for the persistent little blighters. So I was laid up for a couple of days as I started another eighteen day course of treatment. Even though we were getting all supplies flown in, the food was hardly any better.

All through April there was heavy fighting at the north east of the valley and increasingly so in the south west where the Japanese were trying really hard to progress along the Silchar trail towards us. Palel in the south, where we had been evacuated from came under direct attacks as well with some serious engagements taking place.

As an Armourer of 5 Sqdn sometimes there were occasions when duties required me to call at other stations, it could be for collecting parts or signing for armourment etc.

On one routine trip, I was staying at a transit camp for two to three days near Calcutta at the time when a lot of Americans were about when myself and a mate went to a cinema in Chowringhee which had air conditioning and a bar. Generally the common form of transport was the rickshaw but a lot of the Americans used to pay lavish fares to the walli's and they used to know that Sergeants or above had the cash.

When we wanted a ride back to camp the walli wouldn't take us because we were not Sergeants or Officers. We finally persuaded a walli to give us a ride back to camp but near the camp, I told him to stop short of the guard room. The walli wanted 8 or 10 rupees which was far too much, so I threw 8 to 10 anna to him in the dark! He started going on at us demonstrating and the like but we didn't have a clue what he was saying but we were certain that it was some form of swearing in Hindi. By the time he realised how much he had got, we were far into camp.

Sometime in May, myself and a chap called Bret had a day off and managed to get a lift into Calcutta where we went sightseeing. Out of all of the vast array and types of stalls we encountered our favourite was the 'grog shop'. This was for good reason as it was the general custom to sample the wares before buying. On more than one occasion we called in at an Off-license and then we both sampled plenty, and then left, much to the great consternation of the proprietor.

At the beginning of June, I got another bout of Malaria which put me out of action for a few days again. At this rate I was averaging nearly one attack each month. Although I again started the same treatment I was further assessed by the Medics on camp. It was generally agreed that my health and welfare was progressively being weakened by successive bouts of Malaria.

In their wisdom and showing fine judgement in my opinion, I was detailed to spend two weeks rest and recuperation at Utakamund, usually referred to as Ooty or Ootycamund, a Hill Station some way down south east India to aid my recovery. After a chat with the RTO I discovered it was about fifty miles north of a little town called Coimbatore up in the Nilgiri Mountains in southern India and with a serious bit of negotiating I managed to get air transport down to

Yelahanka in Bangalore, where I would then have to get the train to Coimbatore. The last leg of the journey was by a special narrow gauge railway that appeared to cling to the side of the hills interspaced with numerous high bridges spanning tremendously deep gorges and valleys. The line was climbing all the way to finally arrive at Ooty Station where the atmosphere was so much cooler and pleasant due to the high altitude. The actual Hill Station was comparable to Simla but where Simla was carved out of the side of a hill Utakhmund was on the top of its own hill and not quite as big. The views were fantastic as at certain points you could see for tens of miles across the Nilgiri Mountains and valleys. They are also known as the Blue Mountains from the blue smoky haze that is prominent in the area. The camp itself was virtually a small town really with plenty of established buildings like halls, shops, accommodation and a garrison area. Due to the altitude there was an amazing diversity of colour from the flowers and foliage that was so green compared to the plains further down. I had only been there a few days when news came through that the invasion of France had finally taken place on the 6 June. It was the largest offensive that the allies had ever launched with over 150,000 troops and equipment crossing the Channel. There was jubilation everywhere but we all knew it wasn't a 'done deal' yet. Around the same time notices of a 'Boxing Event' were posted around the station for one particular evening. Contenders were organised into a series of bouts but there were a few 'grudge' matches in the programme. Most surprisingly these were to be officiated by none other than General Bill 'Slim' who had been so fundamental in the defence of the Imphal Plain and repelling the Japanese. One bout was between a 15 st. Gunner and a 10 st. 2nd Lieutenant. The first punch from the Gunner laid out the 2nd Lieutenant amidst loads of cheering and jeckling. It was there that I met Guss an American, mainly because he smoked Camel cigarettes and got quite friendly with him. We often passed time having a chat or visiting shops or just walking around the beautiful countryside.

One morning I was out a little earlier and found myself looking across a mysterious sea of mist that created magnificent islands in the distance, just as it was on our bike rides, early in the autumn mornings around Saddleworth moors. Those rides seemed like a precious distant memory albeit with some regret, from an age past. So much had changed in just a few short years but how many people would never know.

Just before I was due to leave (about 22 June) news came through that the siege of Imphal was over and the Japanese had been put to route which was a major cause for celebration by everyone.

As my two weeks of recuperation came to a close I had to go to the RTO and get a rail ticket to return to my detachment at Patharkandi. I arrived at Silchar only to be told that unbeknown to me 5 Squadron had moved down south to Vizagapatam on 22 June, so I was playing 'hunt the squadron' again and had to see the RTO for another rail ticket. The next day I travelled down and as the train pulled in to Vizagapatem station that night I had to wait for transport to camp. In the mean time I found one of the 'better' looking cafes and had a very greasy egg and chips, but it tasted nice. I eventually got a truck to camp. It was the following day that I was informed that 5 Squadron had certainly been there but had gone on to their new posting at Madras (Saint Thomas's Mount Airfield), for conversion to Thunderbolts! It looked like I was still playing hide and seek with my squadron!

At Vizagapatam the water supply came from a well and the next day I clearly remember drinking some of the water that morning. Later in the day, I felt very ill and reported to the sick bay, where I collapsed.

There, I was initially left outside progressively dehydrating for several hours, to see if I died, or maybe not. This was a practice adopted by some of the orderlies as so many people were being admitted and then dying shortly afterwards, so the orderlies left them outside for a few hours initially to see if they died quickly, saving themselves from preparing more beds. I was terribly ill with a headache and constantly wanting to vomit while my stomach felt as though it was being eaten from the inside. The liquid diarrhoea was most embarrassing but I just couldn't move. After some time although I was semi-conscious I was aware that an Indian Army Medical Officer approached me and as I presumably still showed signs of life he asked who I was. When he was told what had happened he laid into the Indian orderlies with his swagger stick going on profusely in Hindi after which some stretcher bearers promptly arrived and I was then admitted to the old Leper Isolation shed with some other potential survivors. Before too long the

MO examined me during which time I was literally quite sick. He promptly diagnosed Cholera and I was rushed to the King George V Hospital in Vizagapetam, where I was quickly put in isolation for 10 days and I cannot remember eating anything. After a week or so I became aware of my surroundings. I still felt terrible but my condition seemed stable and I felt quite grateful and safe in my hospital bed. Life was so different and far from attractive in the surrounding towns and villages at this time as there were many areas of famine around and epidemics of cholera and dysentry breaking out. As I recovered I was able to move around more and chat with other patients and the orderlies.

After a month I started to eat 'normal' food but the disease had left me very weak and undernourished and it was a further two or three weeks more before I was declared well enough to join my squadron again.

After the first week in August I was released from the King George V hospital and almost straight away came across a funeral procession. It seemed a bit ominous at first. Amidst the mourners the dead man was being carried on a Bya (sort of a stretcher) in a sitting position with garlands of flowers around his neck. At the time I wasn't to know what the old chap had died of but I found out that about 150-160 people a day were now dying from Cholera in the town as it had turned in to a full blown epidemic which lasted for weeks. All around the edge of the town Ghats, Indian cremation pyres were constantly burning. I decided to be very careful of what I ate and drank and decided to get myself down to Madras as soon as possible.

I rejoined 5 Sqdn initially at Madras but the pilots were undertaking a conversion programme to the new Thunderbolt fighter planes which was taking place at RAF Yelahanka (Bangalore, the 'garden of India') due east of us. As armourers we had to be familiar with the different armourment and mechanisms on them as well so after two or three weeks I finally caught up with my squadron down there.

St. Thomas's Mount Airfield was only a couple of hours flying time from Bangalore and as it was next to the city of Madras all of us tried to get a ride out there whenever we could. At the actual Mount of Saint Thomas there is a hill with a monastery at the top with a cemetery close by. 360 steps lead up to the monastery and from there the airfield could be seen. No. 7 Radar Station was in the Filter Room across the

Maidan, like a flat plain, close to the Airfield and the Indian barracks. About half way up the steps of the Mount there is a large stone set into the wall with a carved surround. The stone is sort of dark blood red and called the Bleeding Stone. An area of it is black and permanently damp to the touch, leaving a blood red stain on ones fingers.

Every day you could see more of the Burning Ghats about a mile or so further from the camp. The smoke was all too obvious but we frequently got the smell!

At the end of August I was on a visit to Madras and went down with Malaria for the eighth time since I arrived in India. I was well versed in the procedure now but that knowledge in itself did not make the experience any less pleasant or the recovery any quicker. To be declared fit for duty, I was sent for a medical all the way back up north to the British Medical Hospital in Jorhat. Basically I was hospitalised for a couple of days to enable medical examinations and tests to be conducted. I couldn't help feeling that those of us involved were given beds just to keep the place looking tidy. The Medical board consisted of three Senior Medical Officers who did their tests and assessments and then retired to discuss their findings. A short while later the SMO and two Medical Officers came to my bedside to tell me I was to be repatriated to the UK. I had guessed earlier that this may have been a possibility but had not dared to hope for it. They had concluded that 'it would be better for your health' if I were to return by sea rather than air. No one could really disagree when my full medical history was revealed. In the last eighteen months I had caught Malaria eight times, Dysentery twice, Cholera once and been in a near fatal air crash and as I currently weighed only $7\frac{1}{2}$ stone, the case was fairly self evident.

Although I was stationed at Madras on leaving the hospital I had to get a ticket through the Railway Transport Officer to join my squadron at Yelahanka where I would have to get my 'departure chits' signed in order to get repatriated to the United Kingdom.

Once at Yelahanka I duly 'arrived' and requested an interview with the Station Adjutant of 5 Squadron where my situation was clarified. He asked me if I had any money. I felt my pockets and found only a little loose change. 'No Sir.' I said without embarrassment. He put his hand in his pocket and pulled out 35 rupees and gave them to me. I was surprised but very grateful. 'Thanks very much, Sir. I'll pay you back as soon as I can'.

'Very good Butterworth. Just make sure you build yourself up.' he paused. 'There is a Dakota leaving for Bombay in thirty minutes. Be on it'.

I was the only non commissioned rank on that flight which took about 5 hours to our airstrip at Santa Cruz, Bombay. I reported to SMO at Worli Camp where I was told again that I was not being repatriated by plane but by ship in three days. During that time the other blokes being repatriated had got fully kitted out from the relevant stores before embarking. I couldn't be bothered with all the running around involved, so I got a deficiency chit which said I was deficient of the proper kit that I should have and that way I didn't have the extra gear to carry around and when I needed it for cooler climates I could draw it from the ships stores.

I boarded the ship as part of the medical repatriation group only in the boots, shorts and shirt that I was wearing and a hat. I had a small tin trunk with little more in it than the Tankard and wallet I received in Jodhpur but none of us really cared what we had. We were bound for England. After a few days we had crossed the Indian Ocean and were heading into the Red Sea. We had to wait a couple of days at Port Tewfik at one end of the Suez Canal which was about ninety miles long because there was so much shipping coming through.

After we got through Port Said we sailed into the Mediterranean for a recuperative and restful cruise home. There was still a war on but it was three months ago since the D Day landings and the last bit of news we had heard was that Paris had been liberated on 25 August. The Germans were just running out of 'steam' and what with the Russians driving in from the East this must surely be the start of the end. The chances were that I'll get back to good 'ol Blighty and stay there. Going home to Uppermill, to Mum and dad and the Commercial, 'Ol Llewy and Mary his wife and Elsie, my wife. My wife who I haven't seen for over two years. I should be 'over the moon' but pleased though I was, I realized that I felt tired, not just tired but tired within me. I felt like I wanted a home but I wasn't sure about staying in one. I had moved all over the place in the last two years and slept on everything from the ground and straw Palliases in Africa and string Charpoys in the desert and luxury camp beds in the palace. I had worked in the baking desert and the fly ridden stinking jungle. I'd been working with blokes that mostly knew what they were doing, with a common purpose. Blokes that had a job to do and did it. But now I was going home. I felt like a proud hunting dog of old that now the 'kill' had been delivered, was destined to be put on a leash. I was pretty sure that things were going to change, alright. That bit was true but we weren't back yet and hostilities hadn't quite finished round here, at least not locally.

Most of us were in a similar position on board and just wanted a quiet life and a smooth voyage home but there was one problem with our general state of acquiescence. It came in the form of a 5' 10" trooper who quickly became known as motor mouth. It didn't matter who he was talking to, whatever the subject was, wherever they had been or whatever they had done. You could rest assured that he had either been there as well or done it earlier or better or knew someone that had. I never heard his name because no one ever used it. He would just be talking to you until you were compelled to say yes or no to some thing or other. This then clearly indicated that you were talking to him. But there were some individuals he taunted just for the hell of it and a bit too much for my liking, but it was a big ship. Just like a bad penny though, he kept turning up. I'm not sure just how he became seated opposite me at the same mess table on this occasion at breakfast but unfortunately he had and had also caught my shin with his boot as he stepped over the fixed benches.

'Oi!, that was my leg,' I said. Stupidly I thought he might apologize or something, but no.

'Shut up. You've got another one', he said sniggering. 'Anyway, why does a weed like you need so much room, then?'

I tried not to pay any heed to what he said but when he got a bit personal, I felt a change in my stomach that told me a line had been crossed. I stood up to him, a bit slowly. I didn't really notice that as I stood up the room went quiet. 'Oh, you're going to do something about it then, are you?'

Standing up to him seemed to have been a bit of a mistake at first as he was a clearly taller than me but in doing so I'd passed the point of no return. I did have half a plan but I needed a few moments. I leaned towards him slightly putting my left shoulder forward while casually hiding my right arm.

'You are the most obnoxious and brainless gyte I have ever come across.' I said in my standard 'nasty' voice. I was looking him straight in the eye now. His face changed as his eyes opened wide and his jaw dropped almost in shock I think as someone had dared to not only stand up to him but answered him back and insulted him as well, all in one. He didn't realize he was looking at an armourer, one of the 'Heavies'. One who had been humping heavy Browning and Hispano cannons in and out of aircraft for the last two years and been fetching and carrying ammunition boxes in and out of trucks for ages. I may not have weighed a lot but my upper body was like iron and I had now formed a full fist with my right hand. His shoulders gave him away as his right went fully back for his punch and his head turned to the right a little, just as I had hoped. I was primed and ready with my legs firm as I used every bit of effort from my hips and my back to twist my shoulders and drive my fist with all my might on to the upper part of his jaw as I heard something crack. Right on target, his head bounced round a bit further taking his body with it. It was a shame that his legs were caught on the fixed benches because he sort of half twisted and fell back on to the edge of the next steel bench. Cheers from the lads went up all around as did all the porridge and mugs of tea in the vicinity. He didn't fall well and was a bit dazed but I was pretty sure those closest to him managed to get a couple of discreet kicks in as well. With the peak of the moment over I realised my hand was now hurting like hell. If the gimp covered in porridge made a quick recovery I knew I'd be in trouble so I made myself scarce. My hand really hurt but so did his face so a short while later I found him out and in my most threatening manner I gave him a choice, to either report it and get much worse later AND maybe get put over the side, or to forget it. I just left it at that but I was a bit relieved I didn't see much of him afterwards.

I knew I had to see the MO and when he asked me about my hand I told him that I had fallen down the stairs! I knew he didn't believe me but there it was! He checked it out and told me I'd got a badly bruised and strained hand as a result of 'probably' hitting someone. After that incident the voyage continued quite peacefully but loads of different chaps started speaking with me and wanting to be a mate. It was disappointing to find that we were to be anchored off Algiers for three days but then it was only four or five days to Liverpool. When the ship reached colder waters I had to get some better kit and went to the stores. The only kit suitable that came close to fitting was the British Army battle dress which after about four years of 'blues' or 'Khaki' was quite a novelty but definitely much warmer. I cadged a kit bag for my gear as well. We reached Liverpool OK but it took us nearly all day to berth at the docks and a couple more hours to disembark. As we were all looking over the city for anything we recognised I realised that it was just two years since I was last here. There were hundreds of troops crowding the exit doors producing a constant stream of men filing from the gangways to the quayside. In view of this there was always a reception force to receive the homecoming troops. When it came to my turn I couldn't manage my kitbag down the gangway and hold on because of my damaged hand from thumping the bloke. A Sergeant, no less, from the 'reception committee' saw my predicament and came up the gangway against the tide of men. 'Come lad,' he said 'you've done your bit. Let's take that.' He took my kitbag down the gangway and on through to arrivals. With sympathy! I was sent straight to RAF Locking Hospital, near Weston Super Mare where I had a Medical. I was admitted for ten days for a thorough check up, and built up with some decent meals and reclassified as C3 fitness. As I was discharged I was granted one months leave over Christmas period. I went back to Saddleworth and the Commercial Hotel.

I found it hard to believe that with all I'd done and seen and the things that had happened, I now had a new life that I had to start living.

As soon as I could, I did write a letter and repay the Station Adjutant his 35 Rs. I received a letter of thanks for the prompt repayment of the cash but I couldn't help thinking he would have been surprised to see any acknowledgement let alone the repayment!

But life can be surprising!